The new format for *Quiet Spaces* offers rich resources for our prayer life. There is food for nourishment, water for refreshment, wide views for perspective and creativity to develop imagination—ways that lead us into a deeper encounter with God.

ANN PERSSON

Quiet Spaces offers a fresh, creative and flexible way of encountering the Bible and the riches of the Christian tradition. I hope that its inviting format appeals to many seeking nourishment on their spiritual journey.

JOHN PRITCHARD, BISHOP OF OXFORD

Inspiring, informing and practical, and provides plenty of space for people to make use of the scriptures and themes.

MICHAEL MITTON

For anyone seeking to stay in touch with the Spirit and the scriptures, through earthed imagination and inspired meditation, this is an excellent resource.

SIMON REED, COMMUNITY C

Quiet Spaces gives a   bil-
ity built in for people   in
ways that work for th

IAN ADAMS

Quiet Spaces offers a welcome and imaginative complement to traditional daily Bible notes, with scriptural and other Christian themes to ponder and pray with over periods of two weeks. The flexible format is most helpful, as we can use the reflections in whatever way fits best in our particular lifestyle.

ANGELA ASHWIN

Contents

Text copyright © BRF 2015
Authors retain copyright in their own work

Published by
The Bible Reading Fellowship
15 The Chambers
Abingdon, OX14 3FE
United Kingdom
Tel: +44 (0)1865 319700
Email: enquiries@brf.org.uk
Website: www.brf.org.uk
BRF is a Registered Charity

ISBN 978 0 85746 306 7
First published 2015
10 9 8 7 6 5 4 3 2 1 0

Acknowledgements
Unless otherwise stated, scripture quotations taken from The Holy Bible, New International Version Copyright (Anglicised edition) copyright © 1973, 1978, 1984, 2011 by Biblica (formerly International Bible Society). Used by permission of Hodder & Stoughton Publishers, an Hachette UK company. All rights reserved. 'NIV' is a registered trade mark of Biblica (formerly International Bible Society). UK trademark number 1448790.

Scripture quotations taken from The New Revised Standard Version of the Bible, Anglicised Edition, copyright © 1989, 1995 by the Division of Christian Education of the National Council of the Churches of Christ in the USA, and are used by permission. All rights reserved.

Scripture quotations from THE MESSAGE. Copyright © by Eugene H. Peterson 1993, 1994, 1995. Used by permission of NavPress Publishing Group.

Scriptures quoted from the Good News Bible published by The Bible Societies/ HarperCollins Publishers Ltd, UK © American Bible Society 1966, 1971, 1976, 1992, used with permission.

Extract from As a Child by Phil Steer, published by lulu.com, 2012

Cover photograph: © Mikhail Yepishin/iStock/Thinkstock

Every effort has been made to trace and contact copyright owners for material used in this resource. We apologise for any inadvertent omissions or errors, and would ask those concerned to contact us so that full acknowledgement can be made in the future.

A catalogue record for this book is available from the British Library

Printed by Gutenberg Press, Tarxien, Malta

The Editor writes...

 Welcome to *Quiet Spaces*.

This issue covers a great deal as we move from the excitement of Christmas and all our New Year's resolutions (whether formal ones or simply the desire to change) and turn to face Lent and Easter. Many churches celebrate Candlemas around 2 February as a time of leaving the incarnate Christ and turning towards the events of Holy Week and Easter.

Lent is often seen as a time of giving things up. It can also be a time of starting new practices, and of learning more. It used to be a period of preparation for baptism and as such is a good time for reviewing our current spiritual practices and trying new ones. So this year we invite you to explore how and when you pray, what gets in the way, and how you might engage more with silence and solitude—for some a welcome stillness and for others more of a challenge, which I hope you will at least try. Rather than overload you with new ideas, we've then included a section that revisits some of the approaches already introduced and encourages you to reinforce good practices. While I would encourage you to use what is enabling your prayer and leave what is not, I would also encourage you to try something new this Lent; you might be surprised by how God can use your willingness to draw closer to him in fresh ways.

We then focus on the last week of Jesus' life, leading up to the rejoicing of Easter and the resurrection appearances.

To whet your appetite for the summer, we end by looking out of windows and, weather permitting, going out beyond the windows to see what God has in store for us.

Sally Smith

5

Writers in this issue

Bridget Hewitt lives in Northumberland. She is a wife, mother of grown-up sons, and daughter of elderly parents, all of which form the background to her involvement in spiritual direction and group work, travelling the spiritual journey alongside teenagers and adults. She has a Masters degree in Christian spirituality.

Claire Musters is a freelance writer and editor, mother of two, pastor's wife and school governor. Claire's desire is to help others draw closer to God through her writing, which focuses on marriage, parenting, worship and issues facing women today.

Andrea Skevington lives in Suffolk with her family. She writes for both adults and children, winning the Christian Book of the Year award (Speaking Volumes) for her retelling, *The Lion Classic Bible* (Lion Hudson, 2011). She also enjoys story-telling for children and running creative writing seminars for adults.

Helen Jaeger is the internationally published author of five books: *Paths Through Grief, As Night Falls, As Day Dawns, A Treasury of Wisdom* (Lion Hudson) and *Simple* (Scripture Union, 2003). She writes regularly for a variety of publications, including *Woman Alive* and for charities. Helen is also an editor, workshop leader and mentor.

Helen Marshall has worked as a university chaplain and a parish priest. She currently works in a parish in Keswick and as chaplain in an elderly people's home in Penrith. She regularly leads retreats and teaching days on prayer and has published a Grove booklet on St John of the Cross.

Sally Smith enjoys creating spaces that enable encounters with God through leading Quiet Days and creating prayer corners and stations. She has led prayer groups in her local church, works as a spiritual director and writes and produces education materials.

Janet Fletcher is a priest in the city of Bangor, Church in Wales. She is the author of *Pathway to God* (SPCK, 2006) and a contributor to BRF's *Guidelines* Bible reading notes. She is a spiritual director and enjoys leading sessions and study days on prayer and spirituality, Quiet Days and retreats.

Lynne Chitty was Deacon at Gloucester Cathedral and now lives with her cat Eliza in a caravan in the grounds of Mill House Retreats in Devon. She combines leading creative writing courses with times of solitude and has a variety of rescue animals. She is an avid reader and a lifelong Spurs fan.

God within all things

Bridget Hewitt

Natural contemplation

Introduction

Natural contemplation is an ancient concept, stemming from the writings of the early Church. It is a translation from the Greek term *theoria physike*, which was used by the early Church Fathers, and has been at the root of contemplative prayer through the centuries. As we explore and engage in the journey of prayer today, it is good to drink from such ancient sources, for they offer much that may help and sustain us.

Natural contemplation is recognising God at the heart of *everything*. Many of us relate to the idea of finding God within the natural world, but 'natural contemplation' as I am using it here asks more of us! 'Natural' is actually about being human. To be truly human means to recognise God's presence at every turn of life and experience, to become so bound up with God that God shines through everything. Nothing can separate us from him (see Romans 8:31–39).

It is not always easy to recognise God within all things, and we will explore this later. For now, though, as we begin this journey, look at these words from Isaiah: 'Holy, holy, holy is the Lord of hosts; the whole earth is full of his glory' (Isaiah 6:3, NRSV). They are words that many will recognise as the basis of the Sanctus, that great song to the Lord that is part of the setting of the Mass or Eucharist. Rest with these words, wrapping them around your heart or your thoughts; as you go through the day, keep them in your mind, asking God to keep reminding you—particularly when you find it difficult: 'Holy, holy, holy is the Lord… The whole earth is full of his glory.'

Thomas Merton

Spotlight/going outside

Thomas Merton (monk and writer, 1915–68) wrote a great deal on contemplative prayer and is increasingly recognised as someone who opened up and made accessible ancient sources of prayer for the contemporary world. For him this concept of natural contemplation was absolutely vital for spiritual nourishment and growth.

Merton had a great love of the natural world, and even before he had a recognised faith, the natural world gave him spiritual nourishment. As his faith grew, it was not only the natural world that spoke to him of God: he came to recognise God's presence shining out of, and calling to him from, every aspect of life. His discovery of *theoria physike* in the early Christian writings spoke directly to his soul and enabled him to write very much from the heart. It linked with his own experience and thus provided a kind of bridge between that and the tradition of the church. His enthusiasm in trying to explain it fills many pages of his notes on Christian mysticism!

The idea of innerness is very important for understanding natural contemplation. It is not something that can be recognised on the exterior of life. Merton spoke of it as God's wisdom, found in the underlying meaning of things; less, for instance, in the letter of scripture than in its spirit; less in our external ego than our true inner self; less in the external happenings of history than their inner meaning, and so on. He suggests that we need to look at the world and recognise that it is full of 'symbols' which are God's words. It is this different kind of perception that we are invited into, a perception that will then transform our inner life.

So, for Merton, natural contemplation was about depth and innerness, and it opened out into love, wisdom and harmony. It was crucial in bringing to life what otherwise would be one-dimensional and stunted.

Go out for a walk today, with some of these thoughts in mind.

Pay real attention to what you are walking past.

Can you see the world as full of symbols which are words of God?

Recognise these symbols…

Receive them…

Give thanks.

Quietly dwell on this idea, letting it gradually come to have meaning.

Realise how differently you can see things by truly paying attention.

When you get home, you might like to write or draw some of your thoughts.

The perfect land

Meditative

One of the first people to write about *theoria physike* was the monk Evagrius (345–399) who spoke of it as 'the land flowing with milk and honey' (Exodus 3:8), conjuring up that archetypal vision of the perfect land that perhaps in our heart of hearts we all long to inhabit.

Today read the two verses, Exodus 3:7–8.

The Israelites were in slavery to the Egyptians, and Moses received this message from God that God was going to rescue them and to lead them out of a situation in which they felt caught, to a land that held great goodness.

Where in your life might you be caught in a situation, or in ways of looking at things or doing things that feel deadening or powerless?

What would it mean for God to 'come down' and take you to a 'good and broad' place that is flowing with all the goodness life has to offer?

These verses in Exodus give a real sense of God's desire to lead his people out of the deadening situation they found themselves in.

In natural contemplation we find God wanting to enter in, wanting to be born within every aspect of life as we encounter it.

God is there ahead of us, waiting for us to open up that deeper consciousness, deeper awareness.

In every moment of life God is *waiting* and *wanting* to lead us into that land flowing with milk and honey.

Spend some minutes—between ten and 20 if you can manage it—breathing deeply into the present moment, and hear the invitation that is eternally being offered. As your thoughts wander (which they will), try simply to concentrate on your breathing, in and out, in and out. With each breath, you are breathing in God's eternal longing to show you the entry into that land of goodness that is waiting right here, right now. Don't despair when you find your thoughts going off at many tangents: just come back to being aware of your breath each time. God is always there: right here, right now.

Veiling and revealing

Bible study

Maximus the Confessor, one of the great Fathers of the Eastern Church, lived in the seventh century. He was described by Thomas Merton as 'the great doctor of *theoria physike*' and many of his beautiful writings allude to it and can help us in awakening to it.

Read this passage from Maximus slowly: 'In the Scriptures we say the *words* are the clothes of Christ and their *meaning* is his body. The words *veil*, the meaning *reveals*. It is the same in the created world where the *forms* of visible things are like the clothing, and the *ideas according to which they were created* are like the flesh. The former conceal, the latter reveal. For the universal creator and law-maker, the Word, both hides himself in his self-revelation and reveals himself in his hiding of himself' (Oliver Clement, *Roots of Christian Mysticism*, New City, 1993, p. 217, my italics).

Think about the difference between the words—and their meaning, between the outer forms of things—and the ideas according to which they were created.

Look at 2 Corinthians 3:6, in which Paul writes that we are to be ministers of a new covenant 'not of letter but of spirit; for the letter kills, but the Spirit gives life'. Both Paul and Maximus the Confessor are inviting us to a deeper level of consciousness, an awareness that sees beneath the surface of things.

Read the passage from Maximus again, particularly the first sentences. With this in mind, now either take a well-known passage from the Gospels, for example, John 1:1–5, or Luke 10:41–42, or look at Psalm 19 or 139, and simply 'chew' on it, letting the spirit that lies behind it speak to you. (Select only one of these passages: reading too much works against finding the depth.)

Noticing

Going outside

Today is a day of looking and listening. Go outside and simply look.

Look at a tree, a flower, a bird, a stone.

Look at a building, people as they walk past.

Look, but also see.

Listen, but also hear.

Be in the present. Give full attention to what you are looking at, to your surroundings, to the sounds about you.

Life with all its stresses will be going on around you, but just for a few moments this seeing and hearing will allow entry to a deeper level of awareness.

Spend some time simply acknowledging and being thankful for what you have seen and heard.

Inner and outer seeing

Reflective/prayer

Take the final sentence from Maximus the Confessor (page 11) in which he says that the Word hides himself in his self-revelation, but also reveals himself in that very hiding.

How do we uncover the living word of God, hidden within his own self-revelation? How do we recognise God within all things?

Think about your life today, either as it is going to be or as it has been. You may be rushing around from one thing to another, feeling there is not enough time. Or you may be waiting, perhaps bored or anxious. For most of us, most of the time, the likelihood is that we float (or rush) along the outside of life, dealing with what is required of us, getting through our days with varying amounts of satisfaction, inundated with emails and texts and other methods of electronic information, only small amounts of which we can take in. The *outside* of life is what dominates us, dominates how we live our days and organise our time.

An awareness of natural contemplation invites us to see the *inside* of life, to see that our own life has an inner dimension, a depth, that we need to awaken to, that we need, perhaps, to come home to.

As we awaken to this 'innerness', all of life takes on a different meaning, and the word is indeed revealed in surprising places. As the Gospel of Thomas has Jesus say, 'Turn stone, I am there; Cut wood. I am there' (Alan Jacobs, *The Gnostic Gospels*, Watkins Publishing, 2005, p. 41).

In prayer today, use these words from the Gospel of Thomas. Take a stone or a piece of wood. Hold it and feel it. Let it speak to you.

Let it awaken you to the sacred song underlying its existence.
Let it awaken you to connections deep within your own being.
Let it awaken you to the depths of God.

Reflect on these words from Maximus the Confessor: 'Wisdom consists in seeing every object in accordance with its true nature, with perfect interior freedom' (Clement, *Roots of Christian Mysticism*, p. 323).

'God is not here'

Creative/imaginative

To say that God is present in all of life sounds facile in the face of a world in which so many are living amid conflict, poverty, illness, injustice or environmental turmoil. How can we possibly say that God is within all things?

'God wills that we believe we can see him all the time continually, even though it seems to us that we see him very little' (Sheila Upjohn, *All Shall Be Well*, DLT, 1992, p. 13). These are words from Julian of Norwich, the 14th-century English mystic. God *wills*, she says. In other words, God longs for us to believe that we see him at all times, even when we feel he must be far away.

There is no rational way of seeing God where God quite clearly is not.

Yet there is an inner knowing of God that asks us to trust that empty, desolate, impossible place as a place where God may yet appear—perhaps in previously unknown guise.

There are certainly no easy answers, and there is no rational response. But God is beyond rationality, and the insights of the mystics, as these words from Julian of Norwich suggest, are our best guides in this difficult landscape.

'God wills that we believe we can see him all the time continually, even though it seems to us that we see him very little.' Can you make that your own prayer?

Try making a little 'frame'. Make a cardboard cut-out. Write those words from Julian of Norwich around the edge. Keep it beside your bed or on your desk or on your kitchen side—somewhere where you will often see it.

Now try putting your life, mentally, inside that frame. Your life, your thoughts, your whole perception of things. This may seem artificial, but give it a go!

God, of course, is so much larger than anything we can conceive, that we are not actually limiting our lives or our perceptions at all, by putting them within this frame. Without realising it, we may in fact be enlarging them.

Where are you?

Prayer

As we continue to ponder on how we can recognise God's presence in a hurting and unhappy world, either write your own prayer or use this one, pausing after each phrase to let it become real for you.

Where are you, God, in the pain, the hurt, the brokenness?
Where are you, in the incurable illness?
Where are you in the death of a child?
Where are you in the devastation of flooding or drought, of storm or fire?
In war, in poverty; in slavery, and trafficking of human beings; in all kinds of cruelty?
Where are you in sheer 'bad luck', in someone being in the wrong place at the wrong time?
Where are you, God, in all the emptiness and suffering that is part of life?

Lord God, I do not hear easy answers to my questions;
And I know that I must face the emptiness
And yet trust
And that through that trusting
You will emerge
Unknown perhaps
Yet closer to me than I could ever have imagined.

Oh God, you long for us to know you, and to recognise your call through all of life.
Open our hearts,

Enlarge our awareness,
That we may awaken to your presence
And learn to trust and praise you at all times.

And may we, through your grace, become channels through
which love may flow,
And thus awaken your presence to a needy world.
Amen

Holding infinity

Poetry

Poetry can be a helpful way of entering natural contemplation. Think about these words from the poem 'The Marriage of Heaven and Hell' by William Blake (1757–1827):

> *If the doors of perception were cleansed everything would*
> *appear to man as it is, infinite.*
> *For man has closed himself up, till he sees all things thro'*
> *narrow chinks of his cavern.*
> THE SELECTED POEMS OF WILLIAM BLAKE, WORDSWORTH EDITIONS, 2003,
> P. 201

There is very little I can add to this luminous statement. It is simply a case of letting it rest in our thoughts, perhaps using both it, and another famous excerpt from Blake, in prayer:

> *To see a World in a grain of sand,*
> *And a Heaven in a wild flower,*
> *Hold Infinity in the palm of your hand,*
> *And Eternity in an hour.*
> THE SELECTED POEMS OF WILLIAM BLAKE, P. 135

This is natural contemplation. It is to live with deeper awareness, and to know that joyful delight that lies at the heart of every moment.

Sit today with these words
Open your palms to hold infinity
And wonder.

Awareness and awakening

Imaginative/prayer

In the book of Genesis, Jacob, after his unusual dream of the ladder reaching up to heaven, announced, 'Surely the Lord is in this place—and I did not know it… How awesome is this place! This is none other than the house of God, and this is the gate of heaven' (Genesis 28:16–17).

In the 20th century, Thomas Merton echoed that sentiment in a realisation that the gate of heaven is, in fact, everywhere. It is a case of waking up, and recognising!

The crux of natural contemplation is that it transforms our inner lives. For in natural contemplation we are being asked by God to put a different emphasis on life. Once we have been awakened to the fact that the gate of heaven is everywhere, some sort of inner transformation must begin to happen. As Merton says, *theoria physike* cannot be separated from love or from a spiritual way of life, and in this he includes our use both of time and of creation. So it is about how we live alongside others, how we use our time, and how we behave towards creation.

Pray today that you may grow in openness and love.

As you sit to pray, light a candle, and look at its flame, that fragile light shining out.

Imagine God asking you to let that flame of light and warmth and love enter the depths of your heart.

17

Become that light
That warmth
That love.
You are being asked to let it grow within you
To allow time and space for it to grow
And to let it spread out to a needy world.
Pray that you may give space for this love to grow.

Life everlasting

Meditative

Today I suggest a meditation on a passage from *The Secret Garden* by Frances Hodgson Burnett, a children's classic written over 100 years ago. Read it, let it speak to you, and let whatever emerges in your heart lead you into prayer.

One of the strange things about living in the world is that it is only now and then one is quite sure one is going to live for ever and ever and ever. One knows it sometimes when one gets up at the tender, solemn dawn-time and goes out and stands alone and throws one's head far back and looks up and up and watches the pale sky slowly changing and flushing and marvellous unknown things happening until the East almost makes one cry out and one's heart stands still at the strange, unchanging majesty of the rising of the sun— which has been happening every morning for thousands and thousands and thousands of years. One knows it then for a moment or so. And one knows it sometimes when one stands by oneself in a wood at sunset and the mysterious deep gold stillness slanting through and under the branches seems to be saying slowly again and again something one cannot quite hear, however much one tries. Then sometimes the immense quiet of the dark-blue at night with millions of stars waiting and watching makes one sure; and sometimes the sound of far-off music makes it true; and sometimes a look in someone's eyes.

FRANCES HODGSON BURNETT, *THE SECRET GARDEN*, PUFFIN BOOKS, 1951, P. 182

Harmony

Reflective/prayer

Among the many ways in which Thomas Merton brought *theoria physike* into his thought and writing was when he spoke about his admiration for the furniture of the Shakers (a religious sect known, among other things, for the simplicity of their woodwork) to help describe what it meant. It was not only their furniture that he admired for its simplicity of design, but also their farm buildings and barns, which fitted into the landscape on which they were built. This may seem odd to our 21st-century sensitivity, but there is a wisdom in it that should give us pause for thought, for it speaks of a sense of harmony, of human values that we need to retrieve in our busy, speed-driven lifestyles.

How do we learn this sense of harmony?

We are constantly pulled in different directions.

We are often pulled into disharmony with others, and encouraged to let the disharmony grow.

Our anxieties, our hurts, our fears all contribute to driving a wedge between us and between any sense of 'harmony'.

Another of the early Church Fathers, Dionysius the Areopogite, who lived in the sixth century, wrote: 'For anyone who reflects, the appearances of beauty become the themes of an invisible harmony' (Clement, *Roots of Christian Mysticism*, p. 221).

Spend time today with beauty.

Listen to a piece of music that lifts your heart: listen, and really listen; let it lift you from the ongoing distractions of your life.

Or take a picture (a painting, a photo, a calendar picture): simply look at it, spend time really looking, letting it speak to you.

Recognise how different you feel after spending time with beauty, than when you are amid the common stress or anxiety— or even aggression—of life.

Recognise and give thanks for what beauty has given you: and ask God to let that grow within you.

Want it to grow, for it is of God.

Pray with these words taken from Psalm 105:1–4:

Give thanks to the Lord, call on his name...
Sing to him, sing praises to him; tell of all his wonderful
works...
Let the hearts of those who seek the Lord rejoice.
Seek the Lord and his strength; seek his presence
continually.

Let your hearts long to be open, long to be continually praising God, and give thanks.

Cultivating a thankful heart

Claire Musters

Why be thankful?

Introduction

Be honest! Does your heart brim over with thankfulness on a daily basis? No? Mine neither. Not every single day. But that's what Paul says it should do, whatever you are facing: 'Give thanks in all circumstances; for this is God's will for you in Christ Jesus' (1 Thessalonians 5:18, NIV). It's 'God's will' for us to be thankful for, and in, everything. That's quite a tough one, isn't it? We are going to take a look at some ideas that will challenge our hearts and minds, and start to cultivate an attitude of thankfulness within us.

Insecurity, frustration and anxiety, despair and hopelessness are rife among people of all ages, classes and races today. The antidote? Learning to be thankful changes our perspective, and helps us to become aware of possibilities around us. You will find that as you choose to cultivate a thankful heart, your spirit and body will become transformed. Indeed, research has shown that being thankful boosts our feelings of well-being and our immune systems, makes our hearts function well and helps us to sleep better—so there are health benefits too!

Read through Paul's words again, being honest with God about your response to this challenge to be thankful in all circumstances.

A thankfulness psalm

Bible study/creative

Spend some time drawing out the meaning from the scriptures printed below. Focus on becoming aware of your own personal response to them, writing down how you feel and what bubbles up inside you as you read.

> *Let us come before him with thanksgiving and extol him with music and song.*
>
> PSALM 95:2

> *Give thanks to the Lord of lords: His love endures forever.*
>
> PSALM 136:3

> *Be always giving thanks to God the Father for everything, in the name of our Lord Jesus Christ.*
>
> EPHESIANS 5:20

> *For everything God created is good, and nothing is to be rejected if it is received with thanksgiving.*
>
> 1 TIMOTHY 4:4

> *Give praise to the Lord, proclaim his name, make known among the nations what he has done and proclaim that his name is exalted.*
>
> ISAIAH 12:4

> *But thanks be to God! He gives us the victory through our Lord Jesus Christ.*
>
> 1 CORINTHIANS 15:57

Now write a 'thankfulness' psalm or song of your own. Feel free to start from scratch or put together any response sentences you've written to create it.

Encouraging thankfulness

Bible study/prayer

We were made to be thankful, to bow before our God in grateful worship, but sometimes it can be really difficult to do that. So we are now going to look at some of the ways in which the apostle who told us we need to be thankful encouraged thankfulness in others. He wrote many letters to the early churches and often at the start of these letters he gave greetings of grace and peace—and sometimes thanks. Let's take a look at a few examples and see what they can teach us.

Read Colossians 1:3–8.

This letter to the church in Colossae reveals four things that Paul is thankful for. He begins by reminding them of who they should all be thankful to, centring his letter at the start on the source of everything: 'We always thank God, the Father of our Lord Jesus Christ' (v. 3).

He moves to being thankful for the faith that the members of the church have in God, and praising them for their genuine love of others: 'We have heard of your faith in Christ Jesus and of the love you have for all God's people' (v. 4). He then goes on to being thankful for the power of the gospel and the fact that it bears fruit if people believe (vv. 5–6). Finally, he thanks God for Epaphras (v. 7), a faithful minister to whom Paul refers as 'our dear fellow servant' and who was looking after the people of Colossae.

This short passage in Colossians is packed full of the things for which we can be thankful. Of course, ultimately, what our hearts should be brimming over with is praise to God, but we can also be thankful for other believers and for those who are committed to teaching and caring for us, week in, week out.

Why not pause for a moment and thank God for those who lead your church?

Now read Ephesians 1:3–22.

Here Paul starts by praising God for all the blessings he has lavished upon us, including choosing us from the beginning of time: 'In him we were also chosen, having been predestined according to the plan of him who works out everything in conformity with the purpose of his will' (v. 11).

Then, in a similar vein to Colossians, Paul thanks God for those he is writing to: 'For this reason, ever since I heard about your faith in the Lord Jesus and your love for all God's people, I have not stopped giving thanks for you, remembering you in my prayers' (vv. 15–16).

Take a moment to read the first half of this passage again. Allow your heart to praise God for the amazing truth it contains about how God has chosen you and sealed you with the Holy Spirit.

Now thank him for those who reveal his love to you through the way they look after you and encourage you.

Showing thankfulness

Creative

1 Thessalonians 5:11 tells us to 'encourage one another and build each other up'. A great way of doing this is to look out for ways to show someone how thankful you are that they are in your life. Perhaps you could cook them a meal, buy them a small gift or find another way of telling them how much they mean to you. This will do wonders for their inner spirit—and you'll also find that you are uplifted through doing it.

I suggest keeping a supply of nice notelets or paper that you can use every so often to write notes of thankfulness for the people in your life. Today, pick those closest to you and spend some time pondering what you could say to them. Using pen and paper rather than a computer forces you to slow down, giving you the chance to stop and think about the person.

If you have a partner or a flatmate leave them a card letting them know why you thank God for them and why it is wonderful to share your home with them. If you have children, make it a priority to write them a little note and hide it somewhere for them to find later. I have a tradition with my kids: I write a note each morning and put it in their lunchbox. I know that both of them, since being in full-time school, have found lunch times difficult as it reminds them they are away from home all day, and so I make a point of telling them how much they are loved. And on days when I know they have a test or are worried about something in particular, I write a Bible verse or a little prayer for them. I also try to write about characteristics they have that I really appreciate.

You could extend this to people you don't know well. Saying or writing a quick phrase that lets them know you've noticed them and how they make your day better will be such a blessing to them. For example, do you have milk delivered? Leave your milkman (or woman) a note simply saying, 'I thank God for you every time I see fresh milk on my doorstep'—and then make sure you say a prayer of thanks whenever you bring in the milk.

The cross

Meditative

Today we are going to focus specifically on thanking God for what he did on the cross. You might find it helpful to place a small cross or a picture of a cross in front of you to concentrate your thoughts.

Start by simply looking at the cross, and then think about what Jesus dying on that cross has done for you, for your life, for your everyday 'going about'. Speak out a few of your thoughts slowly, mulling over the words and allowing them to sink in.

Here are some thoughts to start you off.

Whether good, bad, enemies or friends, we each deserved to die as we cannot stand before God in our own righteousness.

Through Christ's death we are transformed—given a new identity and new standing before God.

We are dressed in Christ's royal robes rather than our own filthy rags.

We are now free! Free from the clutches of sin and death, free from our enemy's hold on us.

We can now choose to walk in that close relationship with our loving heavenly Father each moment of every day.

Thank you

Creative

Using whatever materials you wish to use (a pen to write or draw with, pastels, paints, photos, magazine clippings or internet printouts, for example), write out the words 'THANK YOU' in outline form on a large piece of paper or card. Now decorate the inside of the letters with examples of things for which you are thankful—perhaps a picture of your family, a postcard of somewhere you enjoyed a great holiday, a scripture that always brings you comfort, a musician whose music always speaks to you, a joke that tickles you, a phrase you use with a friend or family member that fills you with joy, and so on.

You could do something similar on your computer—perhaps

on Pinterest (www.pinterest.com), gathering images of things you are thankful for.

A thankfulness walk

Going outside

I remember one of the first walks my oldest child took as a toddler. I was incredibly frustrated because she was so slow—and so easily distracted. Every little thing held huge interest: a crack in the pavement, a spider crawling along a wall, a lamp post. As I tried to chivvy her along, I felt God telling me to get down to her level and simply enjoy the walk through her eyes. The experience taught me a great deal…

Take some time today to go for a walk. You may have a park or open space nearby—if not, you can do this activity in your local streets, or you may prefer to go for a drive into the country.

Breathe in the air around you, thanking God for the air that sustains not only you but also all the living things nearby.

Ask God to help you see things afresh, from a new and grateful perspective.

Start walking, paying careful attention to all the little details around you. It may be a ladybird on a leaf or a pavement slab, or a bird that flies past. Each time you notice something, stop walking, pause for a moment and then thank God for that particular thing; it could even be a house you particularly like or an ambulance whizzing past—you could thank God for human creativity or the ability to help one another.

Walk for as long as you are able and then, as you are coming to an end, thank God for the experience and the joy of being surrounded by his creation.

Thanking God for all experiences

Poetry/creative

As we have already seen, 1 Thessalonians 5:18 talks about learning to 'give thanks in all circumstances'. Certainly the apostle Paul was a great example of this, praising God even while in chains. When we think about thanksgiving, we don't often turn to those situations that we find difficult or painful. And yet that is precisely the place God wants us to get to—being able to love and thank him, whatever is going on around us or happening to us.

I find the hymn below interesting because it does just that. Rather than focusing on thanking God only for the good times, the writer has juxtaposed the positive with the negative: pleasant weather—and life experiences—with stormy, comfort with pain, roses with thorns.

How often have you thanked God for the difficulties in your life, as well as the easy times?

Read through this hymn, reflecting on the individual images it contains. Try to place yourself in the hymn, and make yourself the protagonist. For example, what memories do you want to bring up and remember? What tears that you thought had passed have brimmed up again? What storms have you weathered? When did you feel God's comfort among the despair? What requests are you glad he denied? In what ways have you felt his hope?

> Thanks to God for my Redeemer,
> Thanks for all Thou dost provide!
> Thanks for times now but a memory,
> Thanks for Jesus by my side!
> Thanks for pleasant, balmy springtime,
> Thanks for dark and stormy fall!

Thanks for tears by now forgotten,
Thanks for peace within my soul!

Thanks for prayers that Thou hast answered,
Thanks for what Thou dost deny!
Thanks for storms that I have weathered,
Thanks for all Thou dost supply!
Thanks for pain, and thanks for pleasure,
Thanks for comfort in despair!
Thanks for grace that none can measure,
Thanks for love beyond compare!

Thanks for roses by the wayside,
Thanks for thorns their stems contain!
Thanks for home and thanks for fireside,
Thanks for hope, that sweet refrain!
Thanks for joy and thanks for sorrow,
Thanks for heav'nly peace with Thee!
Thanks for hope in the tomorrow,
Thanks through all eternity!

AUGUST LUDVIG STORM, OF THE SWEDISH SALVATION ARMY, 1891;
TRANSLATED BY CARL E. BACKSTROM, 1931

Now ask God to reveal to you experiences that are still locked away for which you've never thanked him precisely because they were difficult. Ask for his revelation about them, so that you can see them through his eyes. Wait, seek his wisdom and then speak out a prayer of thanks, acknowledging the part they have played in shaping you. If there is pain or hurt that needs dealing with, sit before your Father and ask him to pour his healing balm on you, opening yourself up to his love and care.

Try writing or drawing a juxtaposing poem or image, picking up on both the good and not so easy things. Keep whatever you create near you for the rest of the week so that you can use it as a starting point for reflective prayer.

A box full of thankfulness

Creative/Bible study

Make or buy a small, attractive box (you can make one cheaply by wrapping a shoebox with pretty paper). Put a notepad and pen inside and place it somewhere within easy reach. Every time you get angry with a person, situation or circumstance, take some time (later in the day if necessary) to write a note to God saying why you're thankful for that person or difficulty.

If you are struggling with the idea of being thankful for difficulties, read through Romans 5:3–5. Dwell on the fact that suffering ultimately produces character and hope, and reveals how much God loves us. Remember too that in Matthew 5:44 God asks us to pray for those who hurt us. And what about Jesus' example? On the cross he prayed that God would forgive those who put him there (Luke 23:34). Your response may be that you can't possibly be grateful for someone who is hurting you, but the challenge is to surrender your feelings to God to allow him to work through whatever difficulty you are facing.

The bits of paper you put into your decorative box can also be used at a later date. Take one out randomly and use it as a basis to pray for the person or situation written on the paper. It may be that you are able to thank God for resolving something by the time you read it again.

Thanking God for the world

Intercession

We have spent time focusing on ourselves and on how we can be more thankful, and also on those we come into contact with regularly. Today we are going to look at how we can widen our perspective and be thankful for the whole world.

You may have lived in a different country at some point in your life. If not, concentrate on a holiday that took you further afield. Thank God for the people who helped you while you were there and for the positive experiences you enjoyed.

Now think about any cultural differences you encountered for the first time. Perhaps bring up some photos on your computer from a trip or collect and put mementos from that place in front of you to help you to remember clearly. Regardless of whether all the cultural differences you encountered were positive or not, spend some time thanking God for his creativity in making such a variety of places and people.

Here are some other ideas.

Do you know anyone who is working abroad? Take some time to pray for them now, then contact them to see how they are and let them know you are praying. You could do some online research to find out more about the country they are in, then pray specifically for any needs within that area.

It is heartbreaking to think about the many war-torn areas of the world. We should be grateful for the safety we enjoy, so thank God for that—and the freedom you have to meet with fellow Christians. Now choose a country where people are caught in war and/or Christians are persecuted. Research online if you aren't sure which country to choose; websites of organisations such as Open Doors (see www.opendoorsuk.org) are good places to start to find out more about the persecuted church. Spend some time praying for all involved in the conflict in the country you've chosen.

Thank you, God

Prayer

Read through each section of the prayer below, saying it aloud if you wish, and then respond in your heart and/or out loud with 'Thank you, God… thank you.'

You may find your own prayers of thanks rise up within you. Feel free to use those as well or instead of the ones here. You might like to write down your prayers and refer back to them at a later date.

God, you made the whole universe—the stars and planets in the sky, the earth and everything in it, and even me.

Thank you, God… thank you.

God, you fashioned me even while I was in my mother's womb and you know all the days I will live on this earth. I can trust you with everything that will happen in my life.

Thank you, God… thank you.

You have brought such wonderful, supportive people into my life. I don't know where I would be without them.

Thank you, God… thank you.

You have granted me endless possibilities; so many choices, and you delight to see me enjoy them.

Thank you, God... thank you.

You give good gifts and long to see each one of us reach our full potential.
Thank you, God... thank you.

You love me so much that you allow me to go through situations that will help me become more like your son.
Thank you, God... thank you.

Even when all around seems confusing and the wider picture of politics, country leaders and wars unfathomable, you are my firm foundation.
Thank you, God... thank you.

One day I will be with you for ever—there will be no more sickness, lying, cheating or sadness.
Thank you, God... thank you.

Develop a thankfulness habit

Creative

I end by including some ideas to help you develop the habit of being thankful in your daily life. You may like to try one out now, and then come back to these pages later to pick another.

Write a thankfulness diary: find a notebook to use and make it a priority to write in it every day, giving thanks for the positive things in your life.

Create a thankfulness tree: this is something you can try over a week or month. It is easiest to use sticky notes on a piece of paper, but you can be as creative as you like. You could make a tree shape out of card and then create branches or leaves separately each day. Then simply write something you are thankful for on the new branch or leaf. If you have a family, you could take it in turns to write something.

Stop and give thanks at meal times: take time to gather together as a household and challenge each person to give thanks for something before you start eating—not necessarily the meal, but something they are looking forward to that day or have enjoyed. Another idea is to encourage each person to pray about how the person on their left blesses them.

Show someone you care: prayerfully consider someone that you are truly thankful to have in your life. Write down the reasons why you are so thankful for him or her on separate pieces of paper, then put them in a container (either a simple glass jar or something you have bought or decorated). Then label the jar with 'Reasons why I'm grateful God brought you into my life' and find the right opportunity to give it to the person.

Regularly help those in need: taking time out to volunteer in a food bank, homeless shelter or old people's home will help you to keep your own life in perspective. Seeing the struggles of others often helps us reflect more positively on the good things we have in our lives.

At the end of the day: recall everything that you were happy for in the day, such as a good lunch or a chat with a friend. Also recall times where you were anxious or had any unhelpful thoughts. Take these to God and say, 'Thank you that I can choose to leave these thoughts at the foot of the cross and focus on the good things I have.'

Thanking God—for you!: look at yourself in the mirror; whether you do this while you are brushing your teeth, combing your hair or taking off make-up, make it part of your daily routine (night-time may be best). Take a long look and think about something you can be thankful for about yourself—a quality or ability you are grateful for, or celebrate something you have achieved that day.

A year of thanks: take time each day (or at least each week) to write out on a piece of paper something for which you are thankful to God. You could do this as an individual, or ask your partner/flatmate/family to do it too. Store the paper with your items of thanks safely and, at the end of the year, pull together all the pieces of paper to create a piece of artwork. This could simply be done by sticking them into a frame that you then hang up. Alternatively, pick your favourites and re-create them in a more creative way so that you have a colourful image of thanks to frame.

Hannah and Samuel

Andrea Skevington

A new chapter

Introduction

Samuel's story comes at a pivotal moment in the history of his people: he is the last of the judges, and the reluctant anointer of kings. His mother's prayers are at the root of his life's work, and the activity of the Holy Spirit is clearly seen in his words and ministry. This ancient story, set in a culture of war and bloodshed, gives prominence to a woman and a child. This is remarkable for its time. We see a growing understanding of God's desire to move and work in those who appear, at first glance, to be neglected, powerless and insignificant. This series of studies will focus on Samuel's early years and on his mother Hannah.

There is much that we can learn. Many churches ache with the pain of not having children, of having few if any young people. Many communities and families know first-hand how destructive conflict between the generations can be. If we open our eyes to Hannah and Samuel's story, we will see glimmers of light, of grace and faithfulness, of God seeking to work to restore people, and a people, to a place of promise and hope. We will see that even, perhaps especially, when our hopes and dreams are slipping away, God works in our brokenness and disappointment to do a new thing. Thanksgiving and blessing ebb and flow through these chapters, reminding us to find peace in God's presence.

If you have time, read through 1 Samuel 1—4:1, 7:2—10:27, 12—13:15.

Hannah's story

Imaginative/creative

Read 1 Samuel 1:1–19, giving time to imagine the people and situations it describes. Reflect on how hard it was for Hannah to be childless, with the whispers from her wider community. Look at the words of her rival, the other wife, and imagine living in that atmosphere. Now notice the kindness her husband shows her, his loving care for her. Notice too her faithfulness in worship. Think through times when the kindness and love of others has been a light to you, and remember times when you have walked alongside someone else. That presence is precious.

See what she does with her anguish and her pain: she pours it out to God in weeping prayer. We do not know if this was the first time she prayed for a child—it would seem likely that this was one prayer among many. God heard; he knew the secrets of her heart, and he answered her.

Use whatever art or craft materials you have available, assembling a variety if you can. Read through the story again, slowly. It may be that colour, shape, pattern and memory begin to form in your mind. Begin to put those on the paper or in the clay or whatever you are using. Don't worry about a finished result; simply aim to express something of your response to Hannah's story. You might find you begin to reflect on your own experience of difficulty, your own prayers, your own hopes and dreams. Prayer does not have to involve words—this creative piece can be offered to God as a prayer.

Hannah's prayer

Bible study/prayer

Read 1 Samuel 1:11–16 carefully. How would you characterise Hannah's prayer? Look at how it is described. It seems that Eli was not used to this kind of prayer. Why do you think he misunderstood, and judged what he was seeing? Notice how Eli came to understand and support Hannah, despite his first impressions.

Hannah's prayer came out of deep unhappiness. She longed for a child in a culture where to be barren was understood as a sign that God was withholding his blessing. She was cruelly bullied by her husband's other wife. It can be hard to pray in such circumstances, but pray she did.

Take this as an example and as permission to release things to God. If you are in difficult times, find encouragement in this prayer to seek God, to spend time in prayer. If you know of others in difficult circumstances, wrestle with God on their behalf.

There are many churches with few, if any, children; they know the experience of barrenness. Let Hannah's prayer urge you to pray earnestly for children to be included in our nation's church family. Pray for Christian influence, for love and hope, to flow out from the churches to the children in our communities. Remember that in many places this is happening already.

You could use Psalms 13; 22; 31; Job 10; Lamentations 3.

Receive these words: 'Go in peace, and may the God of Israel grant you what you have asked of him' (1 Samuel 1:17–18).

As you go, trust that God has heard you and will answer you. Sometimes, God uses us to be part of the answer to our own prayers, so be aware of how you may be led from prayer to action.

In your community

Going outside/intercession

Following on from Hannah's prayer, you could go for a prayer walk in your local area, praying for children and families. You could go on a walk with this aim in mind, or incorporate it into your daily routine. A friend of mine, at home through ill health, uses Google Earth to pray for her local community, virtually walking along the streets and blessing each house she sees.

Before you walk, think about places that matter to families and children in your community: schools, local shops, playgrounds, doctors' surgeries, toddler groups, youth clubs. Give thanks for all the provision for children and families, and for people who give up their time for youth and children's work. Think of the routes that lead to the school. Try to walk these routes, praying for safety and protection. Perhaps there are places where you would feel vulnerable to walk alone. Go with a group and pray, or pray at home, for the children who have to walk there alone.

Look out for signs of lack of ease in your community, and let it spur you to pray for those who are vulnerable. Look too for signs of love and care for young people. As you pass houses, you may notice trampolines, toys in the garden, other signs that a family may live there. Pray blessing on the family. Pray for peace and unity. Pray that the hearts of the fathers may be turned to their children (Luke 1:17). Be sensitive to how God is prompting you to pray.

As you walk past schools, pray for Christian teachers, children and parents. Ask God to show you any ways in which you can support them.

Try to incorporate such prayer into your daily routines. Enquire of local youth and children's workers if there are ways in which you can help. Town pastors often do immensely valuable work with young people.

Whatever the situation in your local community, there are ways in which the church can reach out and make things better.

Hannah's song

Bible study/prayer

Read 1 Samuel 1:21—2:11, and notice how Hannah took time with her child—the gentleness and tenderness of their years together—and then how she gave him up. Consider her thankfulness, her sacrifice, her joyfulness.

Now read Luke 1:39–55, Mary's song, and consider ways in which the situations of these two women were similar or different.

Focus in on the two songs. Take them verse by verse and write out words, phrases and ideas that are similar between the two—using one colour for Hannah and another for Mary. Hannah's song is longer, but you should find echoes as you go along. You may find you have alternate phrases, a kind of call and response arching over the centuries. Read the words you have written aloud, remembering the character of these two women.

Perhaps you can use what you have made as the basis for your own praise and thanksgiving. We want to develop the habit of praising God, of being thankful, whatever our circumstances, and it is good to think back to times when you have been aware of God's help, remember what it was to know your prayers had been heard and answered. It can help to build our faith and trust for the future. Give thanks for particular circumstances, and praise God.

Samuel's ministry

Spotlight/Bible study

Read 1 Samuel 2:11, 18.

This story has already given us a wonderful acknowledgement of Hannah's spirituality at a time when women were often excluded from worship, and now we continue to break the mould by hearing of the ministry of a child. Samuel, a very young child, was accepted, uniquely, as one of those who ministered before the ark of the covenant, a foretaste of the coming kingdom. 'The wolf will live with the lamb, the leopard will lie down with the goat, the calf and the lion and the yearling together; and a little child will lead them' (Isaiah 11:6).

We are not sure of Samuel's role, but the emphasis on ministering 'under Eli the priest' in verse 11, and on 'a boy wearing a linen ephod' in verse 18, suggests that he performed priestly functions under Eli and that such a ministry was highly noteworthy. The linen ephod was a ceremonial garment, and wearing this set the priest apart. Ephods were beautiful garments. We read of them being made of fine yarn in gold and/or blue, with onyx and other rare stones. In the book of Judges, the word is used to describe a symbol that became an idol in itself—a snare for Gideon and his family (Judges 8:27). It was a powerful thing. Here, and in Exodus, it represents the authority given to the priest. While wearing an ephod, he was no longer simply an individual, but the go-between for God and the people. Description of the ephod can be found in Exodus 28:3–13, and of ordination in 29:1–9.

If you have children in your worshipping community, consider how much emphasis and respect is given to their spirituality. Do they have the opportunity to contribute, to minister? Are their views listened to? Is there any way you can support children and families in your church, by prayer, encouragement, practical support? If you have children of your own, take time to listen to their responses to Bible stories, to conversations about God. Treasure their prayers, the wisdom of the child.

The rebellious sons

Bible study/intercession

Our church recently looked at Rob Parsons' book, *Getting your Kids through Church without them ending up hating God* (Monarch Books, 2011). We looked at how the whole worshipping community was involved in this task, not just parents and junior church leaders, how to keep holding out a welcome to teenagers who are questioning and challenging in their behaviour, how to hope and love and accept. It is in this context that we read the following passages: 1 Samuel 2:12–17, 22–25 and 8:1–9.

It must have been so hard for Eli and Samuel to watch their sons as they slid away from God, growing up to use their positions for their own ends. We know that people are free to choose their own way, and that wandering is often a part of the process of spiritual growth. The pain of watching those we love drift away from God, whether they are children, friends or spouses, is deep. Take a moment to lift those you know in this situation up to God.

Now reread Jesus' stories of the lost sheep, and the wayward child (Luke 15).

The difference between Jesus' parables and the stories from 1 Samuel is great. Reflect on the difference the good shepherd and the loving father make. Think about what it means to be sought out by God and waited for patiently by God.

Desmond Tutu's book, *Made for Goodness*, is profound on the parable of the lost sheep: how God seeks us even when we have not turned back. 'God pursues the beloved who has gone astray,' he assures us (Desmond Tutu and Mpho Tutu, *Made for Goodness*, Rider Books, 2010, p. 133). It is a costly, risky strategy, but God knows what he is about. And the father welcomes his son home without any assurance that the son has seen the error of his ways or intends to change. He has simply come home. This is a costly love for us, too, if we seek to welcome the wanderers home, to keep a lamp of love burning in the window to guide them, to reassure them that God is not looking to condemn but to embrace them. We draw strength from God's example to us, to hang on to hope, and to continue to love the unlovely. There are many who have watched loved ones drift and stray for years, who have known the joy of seeing them come home to God.

Pray for those you know who are wandering. Pray for the strength to love them with the Father's love, pray for their safe return, without fear of judgement.

Loved ones away from home

Creative/prayer

Read 1 Samuel 2:18–21, a beautiful, tender story of Hannah making ever larger clothes for her son. It is a powerful acknowledgement of his ministry and also of his growth. She was not holding on to the baby and toddler but was releasing him.

If you have children, consider how your treatment of them changes as they grow. Think about whether there is anything you can do now to acknowledge, equip and support them at the stage they are reaching now.

If you do not, think of the children in your church and wider community, and ask if there is anything you can pass on, any voluntary service you can give to mentor or support.

Maybe you have loved ones away from home: a relative, grown-up children, an old friend perhaps. Take some time to acknowledge what you miss about them. You could then write them a letter or make them a card or a simple, personal gift to show them that you care for them and support them in their new life.

If you have a room in your house that is occasionally used by grown-up children or by visitors, go to it and pray for them, asking God to bless them in their life elsewhere. Imagine their day, their needs; pray for protection and wisdom, health and strength, for the love of God to guide and enfold them.

Hannah's making

Creative

You will need paper, scissors, pens.

Read 1 Samuel 2:18–21. Think of Hannah as she is making clothes for her son each year. Imagine the care she took, her excitement at the thought of seeing him again.

Draw the shape of a small tunic on your paper, and cut it out. Now use it as a template to cut out one a little larger, by drawing around it at a small distance. Continue until you have a series of tunics.

Alternatively, you could draw a series of stick figures, or even a graph, to represent growth in childhood.

You can use these tunics prayerfully. Go back through your own childhood, remembering yourself as vividly as you can at different ages. Remember those around you who supported and helped you at these different times. Give thanks for that help and support. You can write down names or significant events on the tunics. If you had a troubling childhood, you may wish to make a larger tunic to represent Jesus, and then place the troubling times you experienced at different ages on to him, so that he surrounds each one. Pray through those experiences, and seek support if necessary. You might like to contact and thank someone whose support you remember.

If you have time, you could extend this activity. Consider a child you know or a community of children. Ask God what they need at each age, and ask what role you can have in the care and nurture of children as you hold each tunic. Maybe there is a local school where you can volunteer in some way or a family you could support.

Alternatively, charities, homeless shelters and hospitals are often happy to accept children's clothes. Make some enquiries locally and, if you are able, donate some clothes. Perhaps you could sew or knit some clothes, asking God to bless the child who will wear them.

Retelling stories

Creative/reflective

I love finding ways of retelling stories from the Bible for different audiences, especially for children. This is particularly challenging in a secular school environment, where you are speaking to children from a variety of backgrounds, and also to the teachers. I believe passionately in the importance of this task and consider it vital to acknowledge the intelligence and insight of children, aware that they live in a culture that is rich with profound and well-written stories. I always seek to avoid over-simplification and trust the stories to communicate truth. When thinking of writing for children, I acknowledge that they will have a more limited life experience and less specialist knowledge, and try to ease them through the difficulties of the story with tact and respect. To my surprise and delight I find that I often learn more from this creative work than from more conventional teaching and theological study.

Write Samuel's story or Hannah's story, with a particular audience in mind. Maybe it is something you could do as an exercise, to learn the story deeply for yourself, or maybe a door could open for you to use this experience in church or in the wider community. Here are a few pointers, drawn from my experience. Use as much or as little of it as you find helpful.

Storywriting technique

To begin, consider your audience: their age, their previous knowledge. Aim not necessarily for simplicity but for the most skilful storytelling you can.

Read the story you wish to retell prayerfully, asking God what he wishes to say to the younger generation. I consider this a serious and prophetic task. Allow ideas and details to strike you and keep asking these questions as you continue.

If you have time, read different versions; perhaps look at a commentary. Think about how different people have interpreted the story at different times. Be aware of layers of meaning, of the richness of the story.

Close your study books. This is vital. Your head knowledge is useful, but it needs to support your imagination, not overrule it. If you have time, take a stroll, or do something else.

Now, read the story a second time. Imagine that you are the characters and that you do not know how the story will end. What was it like? What was the setting, the sounds and sights and smells? Be as vivid as you can. Stay open. Talk to God about it.

Write. Be tactful with your language; do not explain hard words and ideas directly, but by their context. Draw your readers in, and help them to share what you see.

Reflect on what you have learned.

Hearing God's voice

Imaginative

Read 1 Samuel 3.

Imagine how it was for Samuel, and for Eli, ministering faithfully at a time when the Spirit seemed so quiet. Reflect on where you are in your own life now, and ask God to speak to you as you read.

Picture the lamp of God, not yet gone out, the light flickering in the darkness, dancing on the gold of the ark, and as you think of it, wonder what things act as a lamp to you, to keep you close to God. Wonder, too, what it would be like for a small child to sleep so close to the ark.

Samuel did not know who spoke to him and thought it was Eli. They had a close relationship, working together daily. It is possible that God, not wishing to alarm Samuel, spoke in a way that had some familiar quality to it. Consider how we can hear God. Samuel did not know God and yet heard him. Perhaps we can be alert to God's voice in different people, in different ways. Perhaps we can recall times when God has spoken to us.

Eli heard the rebuke with acceptance and humility. He had heard the message before (2:27–36). It is never easy to accept rebuke or correction. Imagine what it was like for Samuel to deliver the message, and for Eli to hear it.

After this, Samuel was accepted as a prophet, a channel for God's truth and love. Hearing from God led to speaking for God. Reflect on what that might mean for you.

Recognising God's voice

Poetry/prayer

'Speak, for your servant is listening' (1 Samuel 3:10).

How do we listen to God and for God in the midst of our everyday lives? We want to hear his voice, to recognise signs of his activity, his will, as we go about.

Listening is a rare gift. Michael Mitton's book, *A Heart to Listen* (BRF, 2010) is full of insight and help on the subject of learning to listen to each other as well as to God. He writes of the dangers of 'spiritual chatter' in our prayers, staying on the surface, perhaps worrying out loud to God, but not really engaging in conversation, listening, attending to God.

Silent prayer is not easy and is best begun gently, for a short time, building up the time and concentration. If you begin with a habit of prayer in a quiet place, alone, you may find you can learn to engage with God in this way in crowded and noisy places.

So, find a quiet place. Turn off all electronic bleeps and buzzes. You may like to light a candle and choose a short poem or a few verses from scripture to begin. I like the poetry of Wendell Berry and Malcolm Guite for this exercise, or something from one of the Psalms.

Be aware of your breathing, and breathe slowly. Match the words you have chosen with your breathing, in and out. Psalms can match the pattern of breathing well.

Try to fill your mind with the words and your body with the breath, letting go of other thoughts. Do not drive them out but let them pass through. Turn your attention to God, holding an awareness or a longing in your mind.

'Speak, your servant is listening.'

Welcome the Spirit. Keep hold of the quietness; let the silence be warm, tangible, welcoming, the presence of God like warm water or a breeze.

Just a minute will do to begin, and then emerge. Ask God to open your eyes to experience him as you go about your daily life.

Living Lent in prayer

Helen Jaeger

Learning to rely on God

Introduction

Perhaps you feel that you are in a rut with your prayers? Or you sense a desire to re-envision your relationship with God? Maybe the divine is nudging you to be open to new directions, or to renew old practices that you have forgotten or not used for some time?

Or it could be that your prayer life is going well, and you simply want to set aside some time to thank God, to review what's been good and to be open to new ways. Lent is the perfect time to renew a focus on your prayer life.

Some of the following ideas may resonate more with you than others, but it may be worth persevering with the ones that don't necessarily feel natural to begin with. Similar to exercising, a new discipline in your prayer life may feel uncomfortable at first. Perhaps you will feel stretched in unusual ways. Ultimately your commitment to prayer can lead to greater flexibility and freedom in your own unique relationship with God.

We all face barriers to going forwards in prayer—time, routine, familiarity, tradition, personal psychology—that play a part in our willingness or unwillingness to pray.

We also go through different seasons in our lives: times when we feel fruitful and fluid in our spiritual life and other times when we sense that we are more fallow or perhaps even a little arid. These are times when we realise that we are weak. We need help. We may need to ask how to pray. Perhaps we'll ask friends or read some books. Often the last thing we think of doing at these times is to ask God to help us pray.

It may seem counter-intuitive to believe that we can—or should—ask God to help us to pray. After all, we are the ones who are initiating or entering into the dialogue; we wouldn't ask someone we loved to do the speaking for us in a conversation.

Approaching the divine can seem at times so abstract (we are, as all the mystics attest, the creatures and not the Creator) that it's sometimes hard to know how to phrase or shape what to say or how to be.

Commit your prayer life to God and ask God to lead and guide you over the next few weeks. You could make a 'contract' between you and God—for example, 'I will set aside half an hour a day to pray, regardless of how I feel or what other circumstances are happening in my life.' It can be helpful to perform some action to remind you of this over the coming weeks. You could place a stone or clock or other significant object in your prayer space as a reminder, or leave your Bible in the kitchen or a place where it will act as a reminder.

If you feel 'in the dark' in your prayer life, meditate on Isaiah 50:10 (NIV):

> *Who among you fears the Lord and obeys the word of*
> *his servant?*
> *Let the one who walks in the dark,*
> *who has no light,*
> *trust in the name of the Lord*
> *and rely on their God.*

Consider how you can express trust to God.

We do not know

Prayer

Paul guides us when he says that 'we do not know what we ought to pray for, but the Spirit himself intercedes for us through wordless groans' (Romans 8:26).

One place to start in prayer then is simply to say to God: 'Lord, I don't know how to pray. Help me.'

Such a prayer is not always easy, particularly if we are used to being strong in other areas of our lives. We can be certain that this is a good prayer, because countless Christians have discovered, like Paul, that God is 'on our side' when it comes to prayer. God wants to help us to pray, even in 'wordless groans'.

Lent is a good time to embrace our weakness, and to discover that God is in that place with us. What's more, we are reminded that we're loved because we are, not because of what we do or even because of how we pray.

Staying in this perhaps weaker, more wordless place of prayer, we may be surprised to discover that God is with us there, too.

Thank God for your weakness and be prepared to sit in a 'wordless' prayer, that may be unfamiliar, comforted by Paul's words that God is there with you. Could you commit to this exercise for 20 minutes a day?

Lent is often pictured as a time of being 'in the desert', perhaps because of Jesus' experiences in the desert. Yet the Bible also says: 'Who is this coming up from the wilderness, leaning on her beloved?' (Song of Solomon 8:5). How could the image of leaning on God inspire you?

Allow challenge

Reflective

Another way we discover something new and develop greater flexibility in our prayer lives is to explore something different or unfamiliar.

It is true that many of us stick to our comfort zones and at times can be unadventurous. We prefer the patch we know and dare not venture beyond it—almost as if we have a mentality of 'there be monsters out there!'

Not only that, but we may gradually come to believe, through familiarity or routine, that we know how to pray. We think the prayers we say are the ones we truly feel or think. We can easily fall into a kind of mindlessness in prayer. It's a natural consequence of feeling at ease, just as we would with a long-time friend—and that's not always a bad thing.

However, there can be a danger in that we may slide into a kind of shallowness in our prayer lives. For a while, God may let us live with that, but the longer we persevere in prayer, the more likely it is that the divine will invite us deeper—deeper into love and therefore deeper into truth. The experience can be, at first, challenging, although its ultimate aim is to liberate us.

Ask God to lead you into truth in your prayer life and to help you to ask for what is really within your heart.

Your heart's desire

Reflective

Have you ever had the experience of praying and being confronted with hearing God say something along the lines of, 'Is that really what you want?' The first time it happened to me, it was a distinctly uncomfortable experience.

'Well, yes,' I was tempted to say—but I knew this wasn't the truth and that I couldn't be anything less than truthful in the face of Absolute Truth. So I tried another prayer and another—but there was no peace in any of them.

Eventually, I prayed a prayer that I must have initially thought was not acceptable, but I felt a kind of heart's release as I finally prayed it. With it came the sense that this was the right prayer to pray. At that moment, it was almost as if the divine smiled and said, 'At last, now we can have a conversation.' I learned at that time that it was OK to express yourself with honesty in prayer.

Be completely honest in your prayers. Let yourself go and be led by the God who knows us better than we know ourselves. Take as long as you need, as many times as you need, really to get to the heart of what you want to say. You will know this place when you find it.

If God asked you now, 'What do you want from me?', what would you answer? Don't think hard about your answer but go with your gut response. Look for the truth in your answer, even if it surprises you. Then ask God for what you want from him.

The ground of our praying

Reflective

Julian of Norwich, the 14th-century Christian mystic, says in her book *Revelations of Divine Love*:

> Our Lord is the Ground of our Prayer. Herein were seen two properties: the one is rightful prayer, the other is steadfast trust; which He willeth should both be alike large; and thus our prayer pleaseth Him and He of His Goodness fulfilleth it.

Julian makes the extraordinary point that God wants our true heart's prayer precisely because he has put that prayer in our heart—he is the 'ground of our praying'—and therefore wants to fulfil the request.

Practically, you could open yourself up to new ideas through reading something new. Many Christians choose a book to read during Lent. Instead of reading ones you already know, how about looking at the bookshelves of friends (and letting them look at yours) or going to a bookshop or the library and choosing some spiritual reading you wouldn't ordinarily choose?

God's sea of mercy

Reflective

As our weaknesses, our untruthfulness and our shallowness come to light, we may feel the quite normal human reaction to sweep it all under the carpet. We may begin to regret our decision to persevere in prayer.

As we move forward, we may feel a little like someone who's been paddling in the warm shallows of the sea, but who is now moving out into something deeper and maybe at first colder. At the point when our feet no longer touch the bottom of the divine sea in which we pray, we may long for the shallows, just when we are now being invited into something much more strenuous.

But what is the sea that we swim in? God's sea of mercy.

A Polish nun who died just before World War II, Maria Faustina Kowalska, discovered the greatness of God's love and said this sea of prayer was nothing less than the sea of God's mercy. Regardless of her state, she had discovered that she could rely completely on God's mercy: 'All my nothingness is drowned in the sea of mercy. With the confidence of a child, I throw myself into your arms, O Father of mercy' (*Divine Mercy in my Soul: diary of Saint Maria Faustina Kowalska*, Marian Press, 2006, section 505).

Mercy has always traditionally been a theme of Lent. Perhaps it is a part of your spiritual thinking that could reinvigorate your relationship with God, too. What effect would the knowledge that God completely accepts you as you are, here, now, have on the way you pray or the things you talk about?

The Bible tells us that, like for other things we want or need, we can ask for mercy, too: 'Lord, look upon us from heaven, where you live in your holiness and glory. Where is your great concern for us? Where is your power? Where are your love and compassion? Do not ignore us' (Isaiah 63:15, GNB). (Some translations give 'great concern' as 'mercy'.)

Maybe, believing in mercy, you might find the practice of confession to another person a healing part of your prayers, remembering that God wants to embrace you in mercy and wipe away whatever it is that may be troubling you.

Consider making a confession to God and perhaps also to another person, remembering that there is healing in confessing our wrongdoing (1 John 1:9).

Reflect on how you used to pray in the past. Have you lost something—perhaps your enthusiasm, your boldness, your humour, your sense of vision? Is God, in mercy, inviting you to rediscover and reinvigorate these practices again?

Surrender in trust

Bible study/creative

Looking at the Gospels, we find Jesus is constantly sought out by people who are sick and sinful and who are aware of their need of the divine healer. When confronted by the Pharisees, Jesus even describes himself in this way: 'It is not the healthy who need a doctor, but those who are ill' (Luke 5:31).

The weak and the poor are those who particularly seek Jesus, because they have nothing to lose. Nicodemus, on the contrary, must come at night—he is afraid, because he has his reputation to lose (see John 3). They, the ones who have nothing, perhaps find it easier to trust.

Claude de la Columbière (French priest, 1641–82) once wrote a popular treatise called *Trustful Surrender to Divine Providence*. In it he considered the question of whether God could be trusted, even as we are visited by suffering. He concluded:

> We trust ourselves to a doctor because we suppose he knows his business. He orders an operation, which involves cutting away part of our body, and we accept it. We are grateful to him and pay him a large fee, because we judge he would not act as he does unless the remedy were necessary and we must rely on his skill.
>
> Yet we are unwilling to treat God in the same way! It looks as if we do not trust his wisdom and are afraid he cannot do his job properly. We allow ourselves to be operated on by a man who may easily make a mistake—a mistake which may cost us our life—and protest when God sets to work on us.
>
> If we could see all he sees, we would unhesitatingly wish all he wishes. We would beg him on bended knees for those afflictions we now ask him to spare us.

Trust is an essential aspect of prayer.

All too often we are unaware of our own need for healing. We think we have everything together and are scandalised to think that our views, thinking, feelings, even outlook on the world may need challenge and change. Lent is a good time to ask, in honesty: am I being open? Am I willing to let the divine physician touch in me what needs healing or strengthening or challenging? Do I trust enough?

Spend some time creatively engaging with these ideas, perhaps through journalling or making a piece of art.

Embrace humility

Meditative/creative

As we journey along the path of prayer (or as we age and prayer becomes an ingrained discipline of our life) we may find that, rather than prayer becoming easier, sometimes it becomes more difficult.

We may sense, to our embarrassment, that we lack the tools to know how to pray effectively. This is not a reason to be disheartened, because the Bible itself tells us: 'For all those who exalt themselves will be humbled, and those who humble themselves will be exalted' (Luke 14:11).

There is always a temptation, in whatever undertaking, towards a kind of pride, a feeling that we know how to do this—and so, sometimes, we may be given times of aridity in prayer, confusion, a sense of not knowing what direction to go in. Like Paul, we may feel perplexed, persecuted, even put down (2 Corinthians 4:8).

This may be because God, in divine wisdom, is saving us from the trap of pride. 'God opposes the proud, but gives grace to the humble' (James 4:6).

At times like these it can be good to start again in prayer and to meditate with the psalmist: 'My heart is not proud, Lord, my eyes are not haughty, I do not concern myself with great matters or things too wonderful for me' (Psalm 131:1).

Draw the outline of a beautifully wrapped present. Inside the present draw (or put marks, shapes or colours to represent) the good things God has given you. Focus on the small things that often go unnoticed. You may want to write a 'thank you' letter to God, acknowledging his gifts to you.

I said nothing

Reflective

In prayer we are aiming for intimacy with God. God too is seeking intimacy with us. Our pride can be a barrier to that intimacy, while humility can be a gateway. Praying with humility shows that we are serious about becoming supple and flexible in our will. It paves the way to greater intimacy and greater freedom in our prayer life, because it indicates that we are willing to accept whatever comes our way, good or bad.

It's an indication, too, that we are serious when we say, 'Not my will, but yours be done,' just as Jesus himself said (Luke 22:42).

Humility is also a willingness to admit that we don't get everything right, that sometimes we fall and sin and that we are not perfect—and that it will always be this way.

Yet ultimately God is love and, through purification and humility in prayer, we are being invited deeper into that experience of love.

Humility doesn't mean always beating ourselves up about our shortcomings. God does not focus on our faults. The Bible tells us that God, in his graciousness and love towards us, does not keep a record of our faults: 'When you did these things and I kept silent…' (Psalm 50:21). You might want to thank God for the times when he has overlooked your weakness in love.

Be honest

Bible study/imaginative

We've already touched on being honest in prayer, but it may be worth spending more time thinking about this. There are several places in the Bible where we discover that being honest in prayer is exactly the place to meet God.

Look up some of the following examples.

- Jonah, who has survived being swallowed by a big fish and has successfully preached a message of conversion to the city of Nineveh, sits under a tree and asks God to let him die, because he is tired and upset. God sends a plant to give him shade and then a worm that eats the plant. Jonah complains—at which point God talks to him about his mercy for the Ninevites (Jonah 4).
- Hannah, who is desperate for a child, prays in the temple. Comforted that she will have a child, she returns home happier (1 Samuel 1).
- Job, who suffers everything from physical illness to the loss of his family and work, eventually reaches breaking point. This breakthrough moment of honesty is where he finds God (Job 30).
- Isaiah, who admits that he is a 'man of unclean lips, living among a people of unclean lips', meets God at the place of his confession (Isaiah 6).
- Elijah, who, when exhausted and disillusioned, prays, 'Let me die.' An angel is sent to strengthen him for a journey that takes him to a cave, where he meets a God who is gentler than he could ever have imagined (1 Kings 19).
- Mary, who cries and says to Jesus that had he been there, her brother Lazarus would not have died. Jesus is so affected

that he cries with her before raising her brother to life (John 11).

- Ananias, who receives a call from God to lay hands on Paul, tells God that this is the man who has been persecuting Christians everywhere and receives a further answer to his questions (Acts 9).

Do any of the above characters particularly appeal to you, perhaps because of what they said or the circumstances they were in? Choose one and imagine the conversation you might have with them about prayer.

Honesty in prayer

Prayer

Go back to the characters who were honest with God in prayer. Look at the points in their stories where they are honest with God and the words they used in their prayers at that time. Which words could you echo in your own prayers?

Write a prayer letter to God, pouring out what is on your heart and mind. Place it in your prayer place, or put it before a cross, offering it to God and inviting him to read it. Before God, wait for his answer. You could allow God to respond to you as you write his letter back to you. Cherish and hold his words as he cherishes and holds your words.

All things ceased

Meditative

We have spent some time looking at how you could deepen or reinvigorate your prayer life this Lent. Of course, there are always other pathways to discover, such as learning to be fearless when you pray or developing a disciplined habit of prayer. You may wish to consider these as your adventure in prayer continues.

The ultimate aim in prayer is not to prove how good we are at praying, to become proficient (as if we could!), nor constantly to think about how insufficient we are. The ultimate aim of prayer is nothing less than divine union.

We are led by grace, for grace, to grace. In other words, in prayer we are led by love to love.

St John of the Cross (Spanish mystic, 1542–91) says: 'I abandoned and forgot myself, laying my face on my Beloved; all things ceased; I went out from myself, leaving my cares forgotten among the lilies' (*The Dark Night*).

Perhaps in the end that's the ultimate aim of prayer: to have forgotten ourselves in the bliss of the divine embrace. Meditate on this thought.

Silence and solitude

Helen Marshall

A quiet place

Introduction

Many of us acknowledge that in our busy, cluttered lives we need space and silence. In these two weeks we will be exploring how silence and solitude can help us to be more alert to God's life-giving word, and enable us to encounter more truly both ourselves and God.

Silence and solitude, together with corporate praise and community, are part of Christian life and worship. Some Christian traditions have emphasised silence and solitude more than others: for example, the Desert Fathers and Mothers of fourth-century Egypt who left the busy towns and cities to seek to draw closer to God in the desert; the 14th-century English mystics, including Mother Julian and her contemporaries, whose single-minded longing for God was deepened through silence and solitude; or the great Carmelite reformers of 16th-century Spain, Teresa of Ávila and John of the Cross, who taught that silent, contemplative prayer was a means to spiritual growth and transformation.

There are also movements within the Church today, for example, the World Christian Meditation Movement and the Centering Prayer Movement, which seek to encourage us to build the disciplines of silence and solitude into our daily lives in order to root ourselves more deeply in the love of God.

People of all ages can be drawn to silence and solitude. When leading a confirmation class recently, I asked the group when they felt most aware of God. 'When I'm on my own in a quiet place,' was the reply of a 13-year-old boy.

Loving God, still the busy activity of my thoughts and feelings and help me to be truly present to you in the silence. Speak your word to me and touch me afresh with your love. In Jesus' name. Amen

Personality and experience

Reflective

It is important to recognise that our personalities and situations can affect how we think about and experience silence and solitude. Some of us may be desperate for more times of quiet by ourselves, and others may feel we sometimes have too much time on our own and crave more companionship. A time of silence and solitude we have chosen may be experienced differently from one that is enforced upon us through circumstances.

When we choose to spend time in solitude and silence, we may experience it as a time of deepening intimacy with God, a time of refreshment, renewal and joy. But even if we are drawn to silence and solitude, we can still sometimes find it difficult. We can be confronted with attitudes and feelings within us that we would rather not acknowledge; we can become aware of wounds and bitterness, fears and anxieties, selfishness and lack of faith. We can feel naked, vulnerable and exposed, and it is tempting then to run away and plunge ourselves back into activity and busyness. However, if we can offer our vulnerable, naked self to God in our times of silence and solitude, we may find life and healing.

Consider your own response to silence and solitude and how this may have changed over the years. You may want to reflect in a journal on the following questions.

Are you an introvert or an extrovert? Are you most energised by silence and solitude or by time engaging with others?

When and where do you find it easiest to be silent on your own?

What have been your most positive experiences of silence and solitude?

Are you sometimes afraid of silence, and why?

Have you faced times when silence and solitude have been particularly challenging, and how have you dealt with that?

Are you content with the amount of silence and solitude in your life at this point in time? If not, what can you do about it?

Offer your responses to God in prayer.

For God alone

Liturgy

'For God alone my soul waits in silence' (Psalm 62:1, NRSV).

Pray this liturgy slowly with plenty of silence between the different sections in which to receive from God.

God of love, I come before you as I am, and seek to lay down all the roles I play and masks I sometimes put on.

For God alone my soul waits in silence.

I lay down before you my anxieties and fears; wounds from the past and uncertainties about the future. Help me to know your peace and trust your presence.

For God alone my soul waits in silence.

65

I offer to you my meanness and selfishness and the care-lessness with which I sometimes treat others. Open my eyes and enlarge my heart.

For God alone my soul waits in silence.

I bring before you the busyness of my life; everything that makes me feel stressed and burdened. Restore in me a simple longing for you.

For God alone my soul waits in silence.

I remember before you all those whose lives touch mine, especially those I am concerned for. Renew my confidence in your love for them.

For God alone my soul waits in silence.

I give you thanks for the gifts you have given me and the opportunities I have. Help me to discern your Spirit in all I am and do.

For God alone my soul waits in silence.

I offer to you this present moment. Help me to be fully present to you and your love.

For God alone my soul waits in silence.

I pray that the love you have poured out upon me may take root deep in my heart, bear fruit in my life and keep me in thanksgiving and praise of your name.

Amen

The wonder of creation

Going outside/poetry

Set aside some time for a leisurely walk in a beautiful place.

Before and after your walk, you might want to read the poem 'I thank you God for Most This Amazing Day' by e.e. cummings (US American poet, 1894–1962). You can find him reading the poem himself on YouTube. As in most of his poems, he puts words together in an unusual order which can jolt us into a new awareness so that our ears 'awake' and our eyes 'are opened', as he says in the conclusion of this poem. The poem expresses awe, wonder and gratitude that come out of an appreciation of the beauty of the created world and our place within it.

As you walk, try to see and hear with a keener focus. Look at the horizon and take in the scale of your surroundings; the sense of immensity around you, the shapes, the colours and textures and the feel of the air. Pause also to notice the intricate detail of small things; look at the petals of a flower, a tiny insect, or the dew on a blade of grass. Allow yourself to slow down and pay attention. Engage all your senses; look, listen, touch, smell and even taste if you can. Be aware of the feelings, images, biblical echoes which are stirred up in you.

After your walk, you may want to jot down your observations. You could try to write a poem or draw a picture to express your reactions and your response to God.

Practising the presence of God

Spotlight/reflective

When we spend time alone in a beautiful place, we may find it easy to lift our hearts in praise to God; but it is harder to do this in the midst of the pressures and busyness of daily life. Here the teaching of Brother Lawrence may help us.

Brother Lawrence was born Nicholas Herman in Lorraine around 1610, during the reign of Louis XIV. In middle life he was received as a Lay Brother in the order of Discalced Carmelites. He spent much of his life in the monastery kitchen doing work that at first he really disliked. He recommended a discipline he called 'the practice of the presence of God', which enabled him to be mindful of God's presence even in the midst of his work in the kitchen.

In his book, *The Practice of the Presence of God*, his simple message is repeated again and again. 'The most holy practice, the nearest to daily life, and the most essential for the spiritual life, is the practice of the presence of God, that is to find joy in his divine company and to make it a habit of life, speaking humbly and conversing lovingly with him at all times' (Brother Lawrence, *The Practice of the Presence of God*, Hodder and Stoughton, 1981, p. 68). 'I do nothing else but abide in his holy presence, and I do this by a simple attentiveness and a habitual, loving turning of my eyes on him' (p. 44).

Brother Lawrence taught that we should lift our hearts and thoughts to God regularly throughout the day wherever we are and whatever we are doing. 'It is not needful always to be in church to be with God. We can make a chapel of our heart, to which we can from time to time withdraw to have gentle, humble, loving communion with him. Everyone is able to have these familiar conversations with God...' (p. 41).

The effect of this discipline, for Brother Lawrence, was to enable him to do even the tasks he disliked with care and dedication, in awareness of God's presence. Although he had a 'natural aversion' to his work in the kitchen, he was able, through this discipline, to say: 'I turn my little omelette in the pan for the love of God' (p. 85).

How often do you pause in the midst of your daily tasks to lift your heart and mind to God? What might help you to do this more often?

What are the tasks which you find most tedious; to which you have a 'natural aversion'? What difference might the discipline of the 'practice of the presence of God' make to how you approach and perform those tasks? Brother Lawrence said, 'I turn my little omelette for the love of God.' What task would you most like to be able to put into this sentence? 'I... for the love of God.'

Try to do this during the week ahead.

Silence and the word

Bible study/meditative

Sometimes when we read scripture we may read too much or too fast and the words fail to engage us or nourish us deeply. Space and silence can help us to listen to a passage of scripture more attentively, leading us to meditate on the words until they become a part of us. This is the aim of the Benedictine practice of *lectio divina*. Traditionally, there are four stages of *lectio*: first, we *read* the text slowly and carefully; secondly we *meditate* on it, chewing over the words and phrases which strike us; thirdly, we *pray*, using those words and phrases and our reactions to them as a prompt to prayer; fourthly, we *contemplate*, simply resting in God's presence. We might also want to add a fifth stage, which is to *apply* what we have learned to our daily life.

Try this method of meditating on scripture, focusing on the following passage:

Rejoice in the Lord always; again I will say, Rejoice.
Let your gentleness be known to everyone. The Lord is

near. Do not worry about anything, but in everything
by prayer and supplication with thanksgiving let your
requests be known to God. And the peace of God, which
surpasses all understanding, will guard your hearts and
minds in Christ Jesus.

PHILIPPIANS 4:4–7

First, take some time to be silent and still.

Read: read the passage slowly several times, jotting down the words and phrases that particularly strike you.

Meditate: chew over these phrases and what they say to you, reflecting on your different thoughts and emotions.

Pray: bring your reactions, thoughts and emotions to God in prayer.

Contemplate: spend some time in silence, simply resting in God's presence.

Apply: try to apply what you have learned to your own personal situation.

Entering the scene

Imaginative

We can meditate on scripture in different ways. One method, which is particularly associated with St Ignatius of Loyola (1491–1556), is to use our imagination to try to enter into a Gospel passage ourselves, so that we become one of the characters in the story and encounter Jesus afresh.

Take some time to be still and silent, then read the following passage, slowly, several times, so that you are familiar with the story.

*Now as they went on their way, he [Jesus] entered
a certain village, where a woman named Martha
welcomed him into her home. She had a sister named
Mary, who sat at the Lord's feet and listened to what
he was saying. But Martha was distracted by her many
tasks; so she came to him and asked, 'Lord, do you not
care that my sister has left me to do all the work by
myself? Tell her then to help me.' But the Lord answered
her, 'Martha, Martha, you are worried and distracted by
many things; there is need of only one thing. Mary has
chosen the better part, which will not be taken away
from her.'*

LUKE 10:38–42

Now imagine the scene and let your senses come into play.
What do you see around you? What do you hear; what is being
said? What can you smell, touch, taste? How do you feel?

Where are you in this story? Do you become one of the
characters, or do you remain yourself either watching on the
sidelines or taking part?

Focus especially on Jesus. Where are you in relation to Jesus?
Are you close to him or are you keeping your distance?

Enter into dialogue with Jesus. Speak to him and let him speak
to you.

Respond to him. How do you feel and what do you want to
say?

When you are ready, conclude the meditation in your own
way, giving thanks for all you have received and praying through
anything that may have been difficult.

Reflect on the whole experience and what application it might
have to your own life situation now.

Wasting time with God

Prayer/meditative

We can often be 'busy' even in our prayer times. We want to 'measure outcomes', tick off our list the people, concerns and tasks we want to get through with God. Simple, silent, receptive prayer turns this on its head, reminding us that prayer is essentially about what God does in us rather than what we do ourselves. The 14th-century English mystic Walter Hilton calls it 'a holy inactivity and a most active rest' (*The Ladder (or Scale) of Perfection, Book 2*, chapter 40, Penguin Books, 1957, p. 224) and the 16th-century Carmelite St John of the Cross calls it 'holy idleness' ('The Spiritual Canticle, 29.4' in *The Collected Works of St John of the Cross*, translated by Kieran Kavanaugh and Otilio Rodriguez, ICS Publications, 1991, p. 588). In this prayer we are passive rather than actively thinking ourselves; we simply seek to be attentive to God's presence, allowing his grace to work within us. We can sometimes be tempted to feel that such prayer is a waste of time because we cannot measure it; we are not used to *being* rather than *doing*.

As we prepare to pray in such a way, it is helpful to remind ourselves that this kind of prayer cannot be measured by our thoughts or our feelings. It is a prayer of naked trust in God; we simply make ourselves available to him, letting go of our whirling thoughts and trusting he is at work in us whatever our feelings. Our prayer becomes, in Michael Ramsay's words, 'simply a prayer of quiet attention and wanting God' (Michael Ramsay, *Be Still and Know*, Fount Paperbacks, 1982, p. 86).

Try to spend some time attentive to God, opening yourself up to his love. You may find it helpful first to do the following simple exercises.

Sit very still, relaxed, but alert. Become aware of your

breathing; the cold air in and the warm air out. Be thankful for the gift of life.

Lay down your palms on your lap and seek to lay down before God any anxieties and concerns on your mind. Then open your palms upwards in a gesture of readiness to receive from him.

Try to spend 15 minutes in silence. You may find these words from Benedictine nun, Sister Wendy Beckett, helpful:

> You pray for God's sake, you are there for him to look on you, to love you, to take his holy pleasure in you... I am talking simply about being here: the quality is a question for God. Tired or out of sorts, I am still equally myself for him to take hold of me. I will feel nothing of it, that's all.
>
> WENDY BECKET, LEAFLET ARTICLE 'SIMPLE PRAYER', QUIDENHAM CARDS, P. 5, REPRINTED WITH PERMISSION FROM *THE CLERGY REVIEW*, FEBRUARY 1978

Distractions

Meditative

When we try to be silent; focused and attentive before God, we know what often happens—we become overwhelmed by distracting thoughts and feelings. It's frustrating and we can feel discouraged and may be tempted to think that we are just not one of those 'spiritual' people for whom distractions are no problem. Even the greatest teachers on prayer have struggled with distractions, but we can learn from their wisdom in dealing with them.

Read this story from the Desert Fathers:

> A brother said to a hermit: 'My thoughts wander and I am troubled.' He answered: 'Go on sitting in your cell, and your thoughts will come back from their

wanderings. If a she-ass is tethered, her foal skips and gambols all round her but always comes back to the mother. It is like that for anyone who for God's sake sits patiently in his cell. Though the thoughts wander for a time, they will come back to him again.'

BENEDICTA WARD, *THE DESERT FATHERS: SAYINGS OF THE EARLY CHRISTIAN MONKS*, PENGUIN CLASSICS, 2003, P. 70

It may help us to think of our wandering thoughts like a gambolling foal, and of our deepest self, our will and desire, being like the mother ass; if we continue to persevere in patient prayer, seeking God again and again, then our thoughts will eventually return to us and still themselves.

When we are distracted, the teachers of prayer through the centuries encourage us not to be harsh with ourselves but gently bring ourselves back to attentiveness through repeating a simple word such as 'God' or 'love' or a phrase from the Psalms, for example 'for God alone my soul waits in silence'. The Jesus Prayer of the Orthodox Church can be used in this way too; we repeat the prayer, 'Lord Jesus Christ, Son of God, have mercy on me, a sinner' again and again and it leads us into an inner stillness.

Try again to sit attentive to God, stilling your body and mind. Spend 15 minutes in silent prayer. If your thoughts wander, gently bring them back into focus through repeating the Jesus Prayer or a word or phrase from scripture.

Solitude and community

Spotlight/reflective

We may feel drawn to silence and solitude but at times feel somewhat uneasy about it; isn't the Christian faith about relationship and community rather than solitude? However, our silence and solitude can draw us into a deeper sense of solidarity and community with others.

Thomas Merton (1915–68) was a Carthusian monk who lived for most of his life in the monastic community of Our Lady of Gethsemani, Kentucky. He consistently desired more silence and solitude, eventually gaining permission to live in a hermitage in the monastery grounds. However, he also had a great concern for the welfare of society, had many friends and wrote a large volume of letters and books. He expresses the belief that the deeper a person's solitude and silence, the greater their sense of solidarity with others. This partly comes out of his own experience. He records a powerful moment, after years of monastic life, when he realised his deep sense of connection to other people: 'In Louisville, at the corner of Fourth and Walnut, in the centre of the shopping district, I was suddenly overwhelmed by the realisation that I loved all those people, that they were mine and I theirs' (Thomas Merton, *Conjectures of a Guilty Bystander*, Image Books, 1968, p. 156).

He later reflects further on how important and mysterious each individual is: 'Secrecy and solitude are values that belong to the very essence of personality... A person is a person in so far as he has... a solitude of his own that cannot be communicated to anyone else. If I love a person, I will love that which most makes him a person: the secrecy, the hiddenness, the solitude of his own individual being, which God alone can penetrate and understand' (Thomas Merton, *No Man is an Island*, Burnes and Oates, 1955, p. 215).

Visualise the people who are close to you; family members, friends or work colleagues. Focus on one individual at a time; see their faces in your imagination. Remind yourself that this person is unique. He or she is a deep and complex mystery; what you see and know of them is only like the tip of an iceberg, for there is so much more underneath. Marvel at the wonder of each unique person; then offer them to God, aware of his unconditional love for them. Finally, rejoice that all these people are not isolated individuals but are held together, with you, in the deep love of God.

Silence with others

Prayer

Sharing silence together with others can strengthen a sense of community. This is a central feature of Quaker worship, but other Christian groups also encourage shared silence as a way of deepening relationship both with God and with other people. The World Christian Meditation Movement has affiliated groups all over the world who meet together regularly for 30 minutes of shared silence, usually introduced by a short reading. Sharing silence with others in such a way can be a remarkable experience, leading to a renewed sense of openness to God and openness to one another and a deeper unity in the Spirit. The discipline of meeting regularly to share a period of silence with others can also strengthen our own personal discipline of silence.

What opportunities might there be for you to share silence with others, in your family, work or church groups? Find out if there are any silent prayer groups who meet near you and try them out. Experiment with sharing silence with others and reflect on the experience.

Rhythm of life

Creative

Take a large piece of paper and divide it into two columns. In the first column write all those activities you do with other people, for example: work, leisure activities, time with family and friends, church and Christian fellowship or support groups, service in the community. Then, in the other column, write down the times and activities you spend on your own, for example: prayer and silence, reading and reflecting, solitary walks, listening to music. Think about the amount of time you spend on each activity.

Now, take another piece of paper and draw a large circle on it. Choose a range of blues to represent the time you spend with others, and a range of greens to represent the time you spend alone and in silence, and a yellow colour to represent God. Fill in the circle in any way that expresses the balance of your life, and where God's grace touches you.

Finally, review the columns and the drawing and your reactions to them, and offer it all to God in prayer.

Reviewing and remembering

Sally Smith

Lent

Introduction

Lent can be a busy time, when we are bombarded with new ideas and try new ways of praying and serving God. In *Quiet Spaces* we have covered many things so far in Lent. Some will be new, some you may have encountered before and forgotten about, and some will be regular friends. So, before entering the activity of Holy Week and Easter, we pause and review what has been happening, revise what we have learnt and remember who Jesus was and is.

We will revisit some of the themes from Lent so far and some of the ways of praying, and have time to review before moving on.

We will also look at some ideas and practices that fit well with this time of year and will help prepare us for the weeks ahead.

But first, pause. Notice your breathing. Hear the sounds outside and in the room, and inside yourself. Acknowledge that God is with you and sit with him for a while. You may have much you want to say to God, or he may have much he wants to say to you, or you may just sit silently in his presence, enjoying being with him.

Zacchaeus

Imaginative

Already in Lent you may have imagined the scene with Mary and Martha at their home in Bethany (see page 70). As we move towards Jesus' death, we visit another scene from his life—the time when he met Zacchaeus and invited himself for tea.

Read the account of the events in Luke 19:1–10. Read it several times until you are familiar with the details of the story.

Now imagine the scene. At any point in the events feel free to stay for as long as you want or need to; particularly stay with strong feelings and responses, whether positive or negative. What is happening inside you at these points? What are you reacting to in the story events? Gerard Hughes says, 'You may find this part of the scene holds your attention. If so, stay with it as long as you can before moving on, for the object of the prayer is not to cover a syllabus, but to encounter God within you through the medium of the Scripture passage' (*God of Surprises*, Gerard Hughes, 1990, DLT, p. 80).

Make sure you are comfortable and ready to pray, and begin to imagine the scene. There are crowds of people, moving slowly along the path. Look at the people. Listen to their voices. Look around you at the village you are walking through.

Where are you in the crowd? Are you in the middle, jostled along, close to Jesus? Or are you at the edge, looking in? How does it feel to be there? Is that where you really want to be?

Do you talk to anyone?

When do you notice Zacchaeus? What is he doing? How is he feeling? What response do you have?

Watch the story unfolding. Be aware of where you are and how you feel and your response to the events.

When the events in the story are completed, Jesus comes over to you and calls you by your name. What does he say to you then? How do you respond? Spend some time with him talking about what has just happened or anything else that is important to you at the moment.

When you have finished, it can be helpful to replay a video of the session in your head and notice points of strong reaction or emotion. Why did you react like that? What is happening and what can you learn? Where was God in the reaction?

Lectio divina

Meditative/prayer

Earlier in Lent we explored *lectio divina* as a way of praying (see pages 69–70), using a passage, usually from the Bible, and in the silence allowing it to speak to and nourish us.

Take another Bible passage. I suggest John 15:1–9, 'You are the vine'.

Read it slowly several times, noting words, phrases or ideas that seem important to you.

Chew on those phrases, repeating them and allowing the goodness contained within them to come out. Note your internal responses to them.

Bring those thoughts and feelings to God in prayer.

Hold the words in the silence, allowing them to sink deeper and allowing God to use them to reveal himself to you.

Is there anything you need to do or change as a result of this prayer?

You may like to write the words in your prayer journal or put them somewhere as a reminder of what God has been saying.

Repentance

Imaginative

Jesus told a story about a sheep that had got lost and was found by the shepherd (Luke 15:1–7).

In his Gospel Luke tells the story because the Pharisees and the scribes had been grumbling about Jesus' welcoming sinners and eating with them. The shepherd doesn't wait for the sheep to let him know that it is lost. The shepherd goes out and looks for the sheep and then brings it home. The sheep is precious enough to the shepherd for him to notice it is lost. He values the sheep enough to leave the others and to go and find it.

This parable is not just about those who are obviously lost, but about sinners—all of us. Jesus is watching his sheep and looking for the ones that wander off, possibly in search of some tasty food, and then find themselves lost and stuck.

Imagine yourself in a lost place; this might be a real place, a place where you have been lost before, or a situation.

Recognise the feelings you have in that lost place. What is it that brought you to that place? How would you like to turn the clock back?

Then imagine Jesus coming to you in that place. How do you react? What do you say to him? What does Jesus say to you?

Allow Jesus to carry you, on his shoulders or on his back. He is strong enough. Enjoy the closeness to him and the sense of security and comfort he brings.

He brings you 'home'. Where is home? Who joins in the rejoicing as you return?

In a quiet moment in the celebrations, find time and space to thank Jesus for rescuing you. Recognise what this means within and outside the story.

Pulling the plugs

Imaginative/reflective

This prayer exercise is an old favourite of mine, first encountered in Joyce Huggett's *The Smile of Love* (Hodder and Stoughton, 1990, p. 69). As we approach Holy Week it might be appropriate to try it as a way of offering yourself for God's forgiveness and receiving that cleansing and refreshing. It is a way of remembering the love God has for us and asking for a refilling of that love. As we turn to Easter, it reminds us of the reason for the next two weeks.

Find a quiet seat. Make sure you are comfortable and acknowledge your presence before God.

Imagine that you are made of glass. As you look at yourself, you see you are filled with a dirty liquid. What is that liquid? What does it represent in you?

Imagine that at the end of each finger and toe there is a hole which is plugged. An angel appears with you and carefully removes each plug and the liquid begins to pour out. Watch as it goes. Feel the dirty water leaving your body.

You are left with a dirty inside to your body. The angel lifts a lid in your head and washes you clean with refreshing water. Feel it as it cleanses, removing the last of the dirt.

When you are clean, the angel replaces the plugs. Then the angel begins to fill you with a golden liquid, God's love poured into you and filling you. Feel it reach right down to your toes and fingers. Feel it fill you and reach all of your body and recognise the life it represents. Receive God's love as it fills you.

When you are filled with God's golden love, take another look at yourself. How does it feel to be you now?

What do you want to say to the angel or to God? Allow time to speak and to listen.

Gifts

Imaginative/reflective

God longs for us to hear the words spoken by the master in the parable of the talents, 'Well done, good and faithful servant!' (Matthew 25:21, NIV). He wants us to know what we are good at and what pleases him. He wants us then to bless others by telling them what they are good at. We are truly humble when we allow our gifts to be affirmed and to be used alongside those of others to serve God. As we become interdependent, we recognise our dependence on others and on God.

Martin Smith (in *A Season for the Spirit*, 1991, Fount, p. 119) suggests a prayer exercise to help us accept our gifts from God. His experience is that some people find this a difficult exercise to accept, that they are reluctant to begin as it doesn't fit with their view of God. For others, he says, it is an opportunity to hear God's loving thanks. Try it if you can!

> Imagine yourself sitting alone on a favourite stretch of seashore. A stranger approaches along the beach. It is the Lord. As he approaches, you become aware of an expression on his face which makes it clear that his intention is to thank you for all that you do for him. How do you feel? What does Christ say...?

When you have finished, reflect on how you feel, what God said and how you will respond.

Repetition

Prayer

A practice recommended by St Ignatius was that of repetition. He was not suggesting repeating an exercise in exactly the same way as before, but returning to the same place and entering at a deeper level, drawing on the first experience of the prayer and allowing yourself to enter further into the presence of God through it. A repetition is an opportunity to explore a small area in more detail. Returning to a passage or exercise on a different day, we may find we come from a different place and are open to new revelations from God.

You may find it useful to return to parts of prayer that have been particularly powerful or memorable in some way. What more do they have to offer you? Return to the parts you found difficult. What was it about them that made it difficult for you or what was preventing you from going further? Where is God in those difficult places? What can you learn about yourself and about God in those struggles?

Or you may return and pick up where you left off. Where else might this be going; where might God be leading you in this?

Think back over the weeks of Lent. Which prayer exercise stands out for you? Try returning to that exercise, not repeating it exactly the same, but revisiting the powerful parts. Allow it to take you further and be open to following God's lead on where it might be going. It can be helpful to allocate a specific length of time for this and to stay with it for that time. Sometimes it is tempting to give up when there is nothing new happening, but it is in the staying and going through the boredom that we can go deeper.

After your set time, if you keep a journal, you might like to record where the repetition has taken you. What have you gained this time? You might also find it useful to ask yourself at the end of each prayer session if there is more you could gain from this exercise and create a habit of returning when you can so that you begin to find greater depths of God in your prayer.

Purple

Creative

The colour traditionally associated with Lent is purple. In many churches there will be purple altar cloths and vestments at this time of year. Purple is the colour of suffering and mourning, but it is also the colour of kings and so is used to welcome the Advent king and connects the birth and death of Jesus.

Spend some time with the colour purple, allowing it to speak of suffering and of majesty. You could take some magazines and cut out patches of the colour. Arrange them in different ways on different backgrounds. How do they make you feel? What difference does adding another colour such as black or gold make to your response? Can you put the pieces together in a way that invokes sorrow or awe? You might want to stick the pieces in your journal as a reminder.

Alternatively, you could collect purple scarves, clothes, fabric and objects. How can you put them together to create kingly majesty? How can you put them together to invoke sorrow? Respond to the feel of the fabric. Do certain combinations invoke different responses?

Notice which combinations connect you to God. What are they saying to you about God? What is God saying to you through the colour and the combinations?

You could walk round your home or go for a walk outside.

Notice where you see the colour purple. How do you respond to its presence?

As we approach Holy Week and Easter, keep your purple combinations near where you usually pray. Allow the colours to continue to speak to you as you move through the rest of the season.

Baptism

Reflective/imaginative

Traditionally Lent was a time of preparation for baptism, and Easter was the time for baptisms. Many churches still renew baptism promises at their Easter services.

You may remember your baptism. How have the prayers and prophecies of the day since been fulfilled? Look at any promises you made. How have you kept those? If you were to remake your baptism promises today, how would you like them to be different?

You may have been baptised as a child and not remember the event. Look up the baptism service and see what promises were made on your behalf. You may have renewed those promises later at confirmation. How are you keeping those promises now?

You may not have been baptised and might want to explore the possibility with someone at your church.

Use your imagination to visit Jesus' baptism. Imagine entering the scene. Watch, listen, join in. Allow Jesus to invite you into the water. Tell him about your baptism and the difference it makes to you now.

Remembering

Reflective/creative

When someone is about to die, or around the anniversary of their death, we often find ourselves remembering stories about them, or stories they told. It brings us closer to that person and reminds us why we love them.

As we approach Holy Week it is appropriate to remember stories about Jesus and the stories that he told. What is your favourite Jesus story? It might be a parable, an incident from his life, or his teaching on a certain theme.

Come before Jesus and tell him your favourite story.

Explain where you imagine yourself when you think of the story, and what it has meant to you. Tell him why it is your favourite and what it tells you about him.

Listen to what the story is telling you today—it still has new teaching in it.

Allow Jesus to tell it from his perspective. How does he feel about this event and what did he learn from it?

It might help to look it up and read it again—maybe from a different translation if it is becoming over-familiar in your usual one. Read it carefully, looking for the word or phrase you have not noticed before.

You might like to rewrite it, telling the story from the point of view of one of the characters, or from your point of view.

If you have a painting or other image of the scene, take it and remember it, telling Jesus about it and your memories of the story.

Review

Reflective

Look back through *Quiet Spaces*, or through your journal if that is appropriate, and be reminded of the prayer exercises you have worked on during Lent.

As you do so, notice which have been particularly powerful for you. Try to see what you have gained from these and how this might be carried on into life after Easter. It can be useful to look in particular at exercises that have provoked a strong reaction in you—whether that was positive or negative. See if you can determine what was behind that reaction and where God was as you prayed.

Many of you will also have been reading a Lent book of some kind. How has that linked in with your prayer? See if there are common themes coming out of your reading and your prayer and offer those themes to God.

Offer to God the thoughts you have and allow him time and space to respond to you. You might ask him where he was in the prayers and what he wanted to say to you through them.

Did you give anything up for Lent, or take on any new practices? How has this been going? What impact will this have on life after Easter? Think about which practices you would like to continue after Lent.

Rule of life

Reflective

Lent can be a good time for reviewing our spiritual practices and making resolutions about our commitment to God over the coming year. Traditionally it was a time of preparation for baptism, but can also be used as a time of planning the year ahead and thinking about our commitment to worship and service for God.

This exercise is for those who find planning and working to a plan helpful. If you are someone who feels constrained or pressurised by structures, then the 'Rule of life' described below is probably not for you, although you may find it helpful to consider the different areas mentioned.

Take some time to think about what you do at the moment and how often you do it. The following headings might help, though not all will be relevant to everyone:

- Praying alone
- Praying with others
- Receiving in church services
- Receiving Holy Communion
- Quiet Days or retreats
- Serving God through serving others
- Giving
- Reading or training
- Sharing your journey with another

Hold this before God. How could things be changed during the coming year? This might involve cutting down some areas and changing the emphasis in others. There might be ideas that have come up during your prayer in Lent that you would like to incorporate more regularly into your prayer life. Be realistic in what you can include and don't be afraid of taking a break from some practices to make room for new ones.

Keep your ideas manageable. Aim for success and the possibility of exceeding plans rather than building in failure. For example, if you're not sure whether you can manage three or four prayer sessions a week on your own, aim for three, and the fourth—when it happens—will be a bonus.

Write down your plan. Some would call this a 'Rule of life', but try to see it as a framework or a starting point rather than a strict rule. Don't let it become a burden; it should enable your spiritual life, not lead to feelings of guilt when you have failed. Be gentle with yourself when you fail. We are not called to live by regulations but by grace. God will forgive you and wants to meet with you in whatever way you can manage.

God won't call you to account in a year's time, but it will be helpful next Lent to review your Rule and update it in the light of your experience and circumstances. See what has been manageable and what has just not happened. Be open to trying new practices next year and losing some of this year's. Our prayer patterns change as we change, and as our circumstances change.

Passion to passion

Janet Fletcher

Passion: wandering around?

Introduction

Lent begins to draw to a close as we enter into Holy Week (the last week of Jesus' life on earth). The disciples, arriving at Jerusalem, were met with shouts of joy and praise as Jesus rode into the city on a donkey. What do the disciples do in those days before they gather to celebrate the Passover meal?

The Gospels fill this gap with the teaching of Jesus to the crowds and to the disciples. There is a sense of preparing them for all that is soon to come, when Jesus truly enters into his Passion. There is a sense, too, of wandering around, waiting for something to happen, but not sure what that may be.

For ourselves, the first three days of this Holy Week may have a similar feel as we wait for the first of the major services to take place on Maundy Thursday. It may be that in your church there is a Eucharist or time of prayer on each of these days. Do we wander around aimlessly or with a purpose that enables us to prepare spiritually and prayerfully for the self-giving of Jesus? If your church does not mark Holy Week, you might like to find a local church that does and journey with them towards Easter.

The word 'passion' has a number of meanings. It can be the expression of a powerful emotion, or enthusiasm towards another person or cause. Taking the word back to its Latin and Greek roots, passion is associated with suffering. W.H.

Vanstone, in his book *The Stature of Waiting* (DLT, 1982), writes that suffering refers not to pain, distress, or anxiety—words we associate with suffering today—but rather to the many things that we go through, and endure, in our lives; all that happened to Jesus in his earthly life. For Jesus, his passion is more than the pain he endured, but includes his time in the garden praying and his arrest, the questioning that took place and the journey to the cross.

As we enter Holy Week, think about the words 'passion' and 'wandering', and how these might relate to your life and to your journey of faith, especially as that journey now takes you to the cross.

Lament over Jerusalem

Intercession

Read through Matthew 23:37–39. Imagine being there with Jesus and hearing him speak these words. What emotions do you sense he feels as he looks over Jerusalem? In the prayer add in any particular concern you have, a lament to offer as you look 'over' your own community and the wider world.

O God, gather to yourself the people of this world, as a hen gathers her chicks under her wings.

For the areas of this world where destruction is common-place and the lives of so many are regarded as nothing.

O God, gather to yourself the people of this world, as a hen gathers her chicks under her wings.

For the areas of this world where the natural elements of creation are felt at their wildest, causing flood, fire and earthquake.

O God, gather to yourself the people of this world, as a hen gathers her chicks under her wings.

For the areas of this world where there is seen a closing of minds and hardening of hearts to the needs of others.

O God, gather to yourself the people of this world, as a hen gathers her chicks under her wings.

For those who seek peace and justice, and speak out for the voiceless.

O God, gather to yourself the people of this world, as a hen gathers her chicks under her wings.

For those who seek freedom and equality, and strive to bring the daily necessities of living to those most in need.

O God, gather to yourself the people of this world, as a hen gathers her chicks under her wings.

For those we see in need within our own communities, to come alongside them, and to be as Christ to them.

O God, gather to yourself the people of this world, as a hen gathers her chicks under her wings.

Maundy Thursday: Communion

Creative

Maundy Thursday brings to us so many different images that they can be overwhelming, and yet at the same time these are images that are familiar. Many of us come to the upper room each year. We know that all is prepared for the Passover meal, that water will be spilt as Jesus shocks his disciples by washing their feet, and that within that shared meal there is both betrayal and transformation. It is a beginning and a continuation of all that is held in the past and all that is yet to be.

In the upper room, there is communion; the friendship of the disciples and Jesus. Into that communion of friendship, Jesus reveals that communion is about sharing and serving, giving, and receiving.

On Maundy Thursday, we gather in church, in communion and friendship with one another, for Communion. We come to receive the bread and wine which Jesus on that night tells us will become his body broken for us and his blood poured out for us. It is a giving and a receiving, to lead us out to share with and serve others.

I haven't made bread for a long time, but I can still bring to mind the images, scents and feel of the dough and of the finished bread. Bread-making can also be a way of prayer. It takes preparation and concentration, and a waiting as the dough rises, the shaping of the dough in readiness for baking. Once baked, it can be shared with others, in a simple act of communion and friendship, where the presence of Jesus is remembered.

Using either the dry ingredients or a packet mix, make and bake some bread buns. Turn this time into a prayer, reflecting upon the different images of Maundy Thursday, how you come to Communion to receive the bread and wine, and your own particular way of sharing your faith and serving others.

Watching and waiting

Going outside/meditative

If the weather is warm enough, sit outside, or if not, near a window that gives a view of your garden or the outside world. There will be occasions in our lives when we are asked to watch and wait: maybe with a child discovering the freedom of its first steps, a child returning from their first term at university, a relative or friend in hospital, or a loved one as they approach their last days and hours.

This watching and waiting can be distressing as much as it can be a time of excited anticipation. In the 'garden' bring into your prayer your own experiences of watching and waiting; how that felt, or feels now; and seek Jesus with you.

After the Passover meal, Jesus leads his disciples outside to the Garden of Gethsemane. He asks them to wait and to watch with him as he prays to God to be able to fulfil all that soon will take place. We too are asked to watch and wait prayerfully and quietly.

The disciples struggle to keep their eyes open. The cool fresh air, the breeze around them, makes them sleepy at the time when they need to be fully alert and awake. They have experienced an evening that wasn't as they thought it would be. Their minds are full of new teachings and the words of Jesus tumble to and fro within them. They sit and fall asleep.

In the garden the gentle sounds of creation drift across the air, as do the scents coming from the trees and shrubs. They hide the agony soon to come and the cries of Jesus as he brings his fears to God, before a calm acceptance wraps itself around him.

He is ready, but the disciples still sleep. The disciples sleep, but Jesus, then and now, is awake, watching over us and waiting alongside us.

Good Friday: the cross

Reflective/prayer

On Good Friday in Bangor, all the churches come together to process along the High Street, stopping at times for Bible readings and hymns. We follow the cross, which is held high, as an act of witness. We share the truth of the day and give out hot cross buns. Good Friday is the day we are called to come and kneel at, and look upon, the cross of cruelty and death, which was transformed into the cross revealing God's love for us; which then became the symbol of our faith.

It can be difficult truly to enter into the pain, suffering and despair of Good Friday because we know it concludes in the resurrection. How easy is it to put aside our 'knowing' of the story in such a way as to be able to experience it as for the first time?

For Jesus, the cross is not only the place of death, but the place from which there is acceptance of all that is happening to him; Jesus gives himself into the will of God. It is also the place of forgiveness. The criminal and the soldiers receive the gift of forgiveness from Jesus. Do they truly know the gift they have received? Forgiveness, given in love, is never easy. To speak the words may be easy, but it has to come from the heart. To receive forgiveness may also be difficult.

In a time of quiet prayer—at home or in church if there is a watch or vigil—hold your palm cross or a holding cross. Ask God's love to embrace you, to support you in this time of prayer seeking God's forgiveness. Quietly bring to the cross, to Jesus, the things for which you seek forgiveness and seek the strength and love to forgive others. Use the words 'God, forgive me, for I do not always know what I am doing'. In the quietness, feel the touch of the cross in your hand, and in your heart feel the touch of the Spirit, cleansing and renewing as you hear the words of Jesus saying, 'I love you and have redeemed you, you are mine, forgiven and cherished.'

Reflect upon how it feels to seek forgiveness and to know you are forgiven.

Holy Saturday: silence

Prayer

Holy Saturday is often a very busy day, as churches prepare for evening vigil and celebrations of the resurrection. It is a day when flowers are brought into church after a Lenten abstinence. As we take in their scents and colours, our hearts begin to lift in readiness for Easter Day.

There is another element to this Saturday. It is a day of waiting, too, a day of quietness, stillness and wondering. This is the 'silent night' of the Christmas carol, where all seems to be calm and still. Is it, though? It is the day that draws us closer to the dawn of a new day, a day that brings to us God's love and grace and redemption. From the celebration of the carol 'Silent Night' of the birth of Jesus, we move now towards the celebration of the resurrection.

> Silent Day, Holy Day,
> quietly praying in hope, and love,
> waiting, watching with faith in our hearts,
> God's promised Day to arise, when
> Christ, our Saviour is risen,
> Christ, our Saviour is risen.

Before the day of resurrection dawns upon us, we are to wait. Yet much of what we want, it seems, we can often have straight away, and the waiting is minimal. At other times, of course, waiting is long, painful and distressing: sitting at the bedside of a relative or friend who is ill or dying; the waiting for test results; the waiting for examination results or the outcome of a job interview.

In the quietness of a time of prayer, consider the many and varied waiting times you have experienced in your life, and offer them to God. Stay with the waiting of this day before Jesus arises to new life. Bring into the prayer the thoughts and feelings that come to you, and ask God to be with you in all the waiting times in your life.

Easter Day: resurrection

Imaginative

Can I hear the angels singing as the sun rises, 'Glory to God in the highest heaven,' bringing to dawn a new day? Are the angels singing again words of peace and love to all?

Can I feel the trembling of the earth, rolling away all that holds back the shaking of this new day into being? Is this the new and promised day rising now out of the hazy light of dawn?

Can I sense far away, deep beneath, the groans struggling through the darkness and into the light to become a new day? Is this the birthing of new life for all?

Can I see startling new colours, shades and hues defining anew each blade of grass, each bark upon each tree in this garden of all that lives? Does this new day and life bring such new awareness?

Can I now rejoice for the day of resurrection has come, that Christ is risen in the world, and in me? How I wonder at this day, and the mystery and the love surrounding this new day.

Now I feel within, and out of the depths of my life and faith I can say to Jesus risen, 'I know that my Redeemer is living, for this is the truth of Easter Day.'

Mary Magdalene: diary entry

Imaginative

I had slept badly again, tossing and turning all night. Surprisingly, that morning I woke feeling refreshed—thankfully, as I had much to do. Gathering my herbs and ointments, I went to prepare his body for burial.

I wasn't anxious about going to his tomb. I'd prepared bodies before, but this was different. He was my friend and my teacher. He had turned my life around. The streets were empty as I walked with my basket, wondering if I would manage to roll away the stone from the entrance.

It's hard to describe what happened when I got there. It's so hard to believe, and yet I do believe. When I got there, the stone had already been moved from the entrance to the tomb, and so I went in and found it empty. I stood there wondering if I was at the right place, knowing that I was. The first shock came when a voice, seemingly out of nowhere, told me that Jesus had risen. I could see a person, speaking, but couldn't quite take in what was being said. All I wanted to know was where the body of Jesus was, as anyone would, and who had taken him away.

I had to get out of the tomb. Out in the garden I saw the gardener, or so I thought; what a mistake that was! The second shock came when the person I went to seek help from and thought to be the gardener called out my name. Then I knew in my heart. Then I knew who that person was. Then I knew the truth of all that he had told us. I wanted to reach out and touch him, embrace him in my relief and love, but he said, 'No, not now.' Everything had changed; Jesus too. I didn't know what to do next. I felt the presence of love, and of joy and hope again.

Then came the final shock: Jesus asked me to go and tell this good news of resurrection to his disciples. He asked me, a nobody, and a woman, a woman with more than one skeleton in the cupboard! I did as he asked.

Imagine you were with Mary, seeing, hearing and experiencing all that she did. Write your own diary account of that morning.

Questions and doubts

Reflective/prayer

Peter and Thomas were normal people, people we can all relate to. They may have been apostles, disciples of Jesus, but they were also down-to-earth men. Their questioning and doubting and uncertainty reaches across the centuries to the present day. I find them, and Thomas especially, reassuring. They tell me that it's OK to ask questions, however simple and basic, and that it's OK to doubt. It's OK because through the questions and the doubts we can grow in faith and deepen our relationship with God.

They both had faith in Jesus, and at one level they knew and understood him to be the Messiah, the Son of God. And yet Peter betrays him and Thomas doubts. Peter has a painful journey to make. This is a journey to his heart and to the heart of God. It is a journey to seek forgiveness—to forgive himself as much as to know God's forgiveness.

Thomas, who missed the first appearance of the risen Jesus, says he has to see him with his own eyes before he will believe.

He cannot trust the words, the testimony, of the other disciples. His journey is also a journey to his heart, a journey towards acceptance, trust and a belief in God that does not need the actual and visible proof of the risen Jesus to be seen before he will believe.

In the world, and in our lives, we need Peter and Thomas. They remind us of our own human frailty and the wavering of our faith at times. They are human as we are, vulnerable and puzzled by what God is doing and has done.

In a time of quiet prayer, look at your own journey in life and faith, and reflect upon the 'Peter' and 'Thomas' within you. What are your doubts, times of betraying the faith you have, and questions you would like to have answered? How have your times of doubting and questions affected, challenged and deepened your faith?

On the road

Meditative

In Luke 24:13–35 we read the story of two disciples who experience an encounter with Jesus that turns their lives around. Through that encounter they move from sorrow to joy, from bewilderment to realisation, and from questioning to a deeper understanding.

This may be a familiar story to you, but read through the verses again.

There are two journeys taking place within this story. A physical journey, as the two disciples walk the seven miles to Emmaus, and a spiritual journey, as the disciples come to walk the way of Jesus in faith.

The story begins with the disciples talking together as they walk home. They try to make sense of the events of the last few days. A stranger they do not recognise joins them and they recount all that has happened to Jesus. Their hearts are warmed as, taking them back to Moses, he seeks to help them understand. Yet only when he breaks the bread do the disciples know that the man with them on their walk home is Jesus. With understanding, they hurry back to share this with the other disciples.

In a time of quiet prayer, imagine that Jesus sits in the chair near to you, waiting and ready to be with you in conversation. Reflect upon the story of the disciples and their journey: what seems to be important to you and what questions you would have asked Jesus. Bring those questions to Jesus in prayer and in the stillness hear his words. Ask, too, how you may share the understanding and faith that you have.

Picnic on the beach

Reflective

I remember having picnics on the beach with my parents and sisters when I was young. Usually, we had sandwiches and cakes, made at home and carefully packed into bags and boxes. I don't remember having a barbecue or eating fish, but I do remember the care that had to be taken to ensure the sand was kept away from the sandwiches!

The picnic to which the disciples find themselves invited was an invitation they were not expecting (see John 21:4–19). Having fished all night, they were tired and disappointed at the lack of fish caught. A voice came to them across the waters, telling them to try again, which they did, and they were surprised by their catch. Looking to the shore, Peter realises who it is next to the fire on the beach, and why they have caught so many fish.

Once ashore, they come together and eat fish and bread for breakfast. They talk quietly as they eat. Peter is called away from the crowd by Jesus. He is surprised that Jesus wants to know whether Peter loves him. 'Of course I do,' Peter answers, not once but three times. At that last affirmation of his love, Peter senses a release from the three times he denied knowing who Jesus was. Now, in his love, he will follow and serve as called to, even unto death.

In our story of faith, it may not be at a picnic on the beach where we hear Jesus ask us if we love him. Think about your story, and how you first came to know Jesus' love for you, and how you responded to that love.

Passion: making disciples

Reflective

At the end of the Gospel of Matthew we read the Great Commission (28:18–20). Jesus is with his disciples and sends them out to preach and teach and baptise, to share their faith with others and so draw them into the love of God, who is with them always.

There is no more wandering aimlessly about; they have been commissioned, sent out to wander with a purpose across the country and further afield, spreading the good news of Jesus. Although some will suffer as they carry out this commission, the passion they carry with them is that of love—a passionate love of, and belief in Jesus.

Over the days and years that follow, they will each discover the mission they are called to, one which they will fulfil as best they can. In doing so, the passion they feel in their hearts comes to warm the hearts of others; and so on until this day. We have the commission to continue to share in the passion of Jesus, each of us in our own way, as his disciples in today's world.

What does being a disciple mean to you? What is your own 'passion' or way of knowing God's love for you and sharing that love with others?

Passionate God,
open my heart to receive your love,
open my ears to hear your call to me,
open my eyes to see how I can serve you in the world,
open my hands to welcome others in your name,
open my life to the passion you give to be a disciple in your name.
And be with me always, to the end of the age.
Amen

Windows

Lynne Chitty

View from the window

Reflective

The day begins in my caravan, which I share with my cat Eliza, at 4 am as I light a candle, welcome the dawn and watch and listen as the birds and the garden wake up. Bats go back to the barn, pigeons come out and the rhythm of creation helps me to build a rhythm of prayer and life for myself. Then I feed the animals and go over to the kitchen to make bread. It has been a real joy to discover the prayerfulness of kneading dough with yeast that can't be hurried. It is a living parable as the muddle of ingredients becomes a beautiful loaf. Such it is in community and church and family.

After morning prayer, the day is filled with a mixture of practical work, reading, writing and watching the abundant wildlife; with time also to play and do those things that get pushed out when we become hemmed in by busyness, responsibilities and expectations.

My day ends with Compline as I listen to the birds singing out their night prayers and watch light and darkness kiss each other like peace and righteousness. The bats come out and the pigeons go home and I blow my candle out, trusting in the enduring faithfulness of God.

The more time I spend in solitude and silence, the deeper I feel drawn into the heart of humanity, and the sense of holding the suffering of the world in my own heart becomes more urgent.

Amidst the beauty I see from my caravan window I see baby birds that fall prey to predators and rabbits with myxomatosis. The reality of Good Friday and the hope of Easter Day are my breathing in and out; they are music and they are a silent scream. They both fill and empty me. Gratitude for the gift of life, and the realisation of how fragile and how precious it is, encourages me to go on day by day seeking God everywhere and in everything and to build a sacred rhythm that sustains and strengthens.

What are your first thoughts in the morning? Offer them as your prayer, however disjointed they are or however you feel.

When you draw back your curtains, what do you see?

Is there a rhythm to your life? If not, how might you balance busyness and rest?

As you look out of your window, are you able to hold prayerfully together the suffering of Good Friday and the hope of Easter Day?

Window of a new day

Poetry

At the beginning of the day, light a candle and sit quietly. Prayerfully imagine yourself opening the window of your mind to let God's light show you all that you need for the day ahead.

Open the window of your heart to hear the words God would speak to you today.

Reflect on the following poem.

Sacred Rhythm

*As dawn gently draws back the veil of night's darkness
and the window of a new morning stands open
Be bold.*

Let in a new experience,
A new opportunity
A new NOW.
Embrace the light that awakens you
And let thankfulness shine within as brightly as the first
candle that you light.
Let it be as the pen that etches the longings of your heart
on the crisp new page of a breaking day.

Let trust be the silence that sings quietly in your soul as you
breathe in and out.
Leave space between each word, each sigh, each task.
Space enough for presence.
Enriching, healing, guiding your steps moment by moment,
hour by hour towards the closing of the day.

When dusk gently closes the window and today lays down
her tools and slips, unafraid, into the welcoming arms of
the night stars of tomorrow.

Use each day wisely.
Make time
Be still
Honour all you meet
Savour all you eat
Befriend yourself
Laugh at yourself
Sing with the birds
Touch the earth
And let the sacredness of all that you are
Be the pillow on which you rest your head
Until dawn gently draws back the veil of night's darkness,
and the window of a new morning is opened.

For you, is each new day just another day to get through, or a new beginning?

Treasure in a field

Reflective

Stinging nettles don't have many redeeming features (apart from making good soup), but they are a breeding ground for butterflies and a source of food for caterpillars. One of the joys of the longer spring days is watching caterpillars chomping their way through leaf after leaf, leaving only the skeleton behind.

From my caravan, the field I live in looks at first glance like a scruffy, neglected wilderness, but if you walk slowly and look closely, you will find these wriggling communities of tiny black creatures—treasure easily missed. Dozens of them journeying into a new way of being, embracing colour and flight as they emerge from their cocoons, leaving behind bits of themselves no longer needed in their lives as butterflies. Although they don't go far from their beloved nettles, their whole experience of life will be transformed as they dance in the air with an abandonment I can only marvel at.

I'm reminded of a story…

The man whispered: 'God, speak to me,' and a meadow lark sang.
But the man did not hear it.
So the man yelled: 'God, speak to me,' and the thunder rolled across the sky.
But the man did not listen.
So the man cried out in despair: 'Touch me, God, and let me know you are here.'

Whereupon God reached down and touched the man.
But the man brushed the butterfly away and walked on.

Take a moment today to look for beauty in unexpected places.
   Reflect on what it might be time to leave behind.
   What feeds you?
   Are you ready to stretch out your wings?
   What might it take to transform your experience of daily living?

Dirty windows

Creative/prayer

Mistaking a magpie for a jay was rather worrying, until I realised how dirty my caravan windows had got! Jesus said, 'The eyes are the windows into your body' (Matthew 6:22, *The Message*), and this started me wondering whether my inner windows needed cleaning as well. In many churches going to confession isn't that popular now, but I wonder whether confession isn't perhaps a spiritual equivalent of cleaning the windows: naming those things that blur our vision and stop us seeing clearly. Things like bitterness and jealousy can affect how we see others. Greed and possessiveness can prevent us from seeing how we might share with others. Fear and mistrust might prevent us from seeing a way forward. Making an idol of busyness might prevent us from seeing that we need to make time to be still and to pray. Pride or self-importance may prevent us from seeing that we need the help of others. We may be letting past mistakes define us and blind us to new possibilities, new confidence and new beginnings.

   How about doing a bit of window cleaning today? Read Psalm 51 slowly and out loud. Write down on sticky notes those things that you know are affecting how you see yourself and others. Stick them on a window, then take them off one by one. As you do so, offer each one to God, then screw it up and throw it away.

Gracious God, cleanse me of all that mars your image in me and distorts my view of your people and your world. May I see with your clarity, your compassion, and your humility. In Jesus' name I pray. Amen

Thank God for the gift of forgiveness.

Special views

Prayer

One of my favourite windows is in an upstairs room at a friend's house in Sidmouth, where I go for a holiday once a year. You can see the sea in the distance—water and sky wrapping around each other in the mist of the morning, complemented by the call of the gulls; disappearing in the greyness of rain or vividly blue when the sun is shining, calling me to get up and go and swim, or at least paddle my feet. To the left you can see a scattering of houses on a hill. Morning and evening I say these prayers as the lights come on in the houses at the start of the day and busy lives begin, and then go off at night until the hillside is in darkness and sleep calls everyone to rest.

As the light breaks through the darkness and a new day is born, so we pray, Lord Jesus,
for the light of your peace into the darkness of violence
for the light of trust into the darkness of broken relationships
for the light of hope into the darkness of unemployment and poverty

for the light of perseverance in the darkness of weariness
for the light of healing into the darkness of suffering
for the light of integrity into the darkness of temptation
for the light of courage for all those who face today in the darkness of dread
for the light of your kingdom into all the places of darkness in our lives and world
Amen

As darkness falls, God of our tiredness—bless us with your sleep
When things left undone weigh heavily on our mind—bless us with your peace
Dwell with us this night, God of our longing, and keep us safe in Jesus' name
Amen

Where is your favourite window?
  How can the view help you to pray?

Glimpses on a journey

Intercession

I always get excited about going on train journeys and have usually eaten my packed lunch by the time we get out of the station! One of the best things about travelling is that you get to glimpse so much in a very short space of time. In gardens that back on to the train track you see washing hanging out, trampolines, discarded furniture, tidy allotments, weeds gone wild, cats sitting on gate posts, pigeons perched on fences—a great diversity of lives passed by in the blinking of an eye. It is quite awe-inspiring to think that God knows the names of everyone in those homes, their hopes, their fears, their grief, their joys.

Travelling is a good opportunity to pray. Whether you are on a train or coach, a passenger in a car or just walking, you can reach out to those you pass by and ask God's blessing on them.

Find a local map and imagine all the journeys those in your area are making. To work, to school, to the doctor...

Journey with them in prayer and ask God for a sense of his presence in your journey through this day.

If you can, walk around your local area and pray for all those whose homes you pass by. Imagine Jesus walking with you. Ask God to open your eyes to see as he sees.

Windows of longing

Imaginative/intercession

Many look out of windows with aching hearts, with longing, willing a missing family member to come home, wishing they still had the physical fitness or confidence or mental ability to go out as they once did. For many the world is 'out there' and they sit alone with their pain, their regret, their grief. Many look out from places they do not want to be, some wondering if they will ever go home, some knowing for sure that they won't.

The following is a reflection on how the mother of the prodigal son might have felt, based on the story in Luke 15:11–32.

Did his mother look out of the window each morning, go out day by day, stand and watch and wait, hoping her youngest son would come back—today?

Did her heart leap each time she saw a figure in the distance, and break when it was another mother's son?

Did she weep for her husband as he looked away from the empty place at the table, meal after meal? Did she blame him?

And did her anguished prayers at last reach her boy and touch the separation in his soul, kindling some small vestige of hope, a flickering faith that saw in a moment, almost too late, his wretchedness and the pride that kept him imprisoned with the pigs?

Did her calling prompt his journey home?

Later, when he became a father himself and realised what pain he had caused, did he seek out his ageing mother and embrace her, finally understanding the cost of love?

Did he tell his own son of his failing?

And which mother's son is feeding the pigs now?

Do you have a window inside you where you are afraid to draw back the curtains and look out?

Do you feel trapped behind a window or a sense of life being 'out there', passing you by?

How might you change the situation?

Might God be waiting for you to come to your senses and to start your journey back home?

God of our longing, we entrust to you today those whose view of the world is through windows of grief and pain and loneliness. Bless them and us with courage, comfort and the assurance of your love. We pray in Jesus' name. Amen

Windows tell stories

Poetry/meditative

Since medieval times artists and craftsmen have depicted biblical stories in the stained-glass windows of cathedrals and churches. From the outside they are dark and drab with meaningless lead lines intersecting them and we cannot guess their significance or imagine the glory of their hues. Until, as Eric Milner-White

(1884–1963, Dean of York, 1941–63) wrote, 'we step inside and then all is transformed' (quoted in David Welander, *The Stained Glass of Gloucester Cathedral*, 1985). They come to life; they tell their stories, and they point beyond themselves and invite us on a journey of discovery.

One such window is in the Blue Chapel at Gloucester Cathedral. In between two windows celebrating creation, Thomas Denny has created a striking and moving picture of the encounter of Thomas with the risen Christ. For half an hour a day I sat in silent prayer with that as the backdrop and was drawn deeper and deeper into that life-changing moment for the disciple whose 'doubts' became a precious gift to those who come after him.

This is the poem I wrote sitting there one day.

> *My Lord, my God, forgive me,*
> *I thought that you were dead,*
> *I couldn't stand their laughter*
> *So I turned away and fled.*
>
> *I felt those bloody, spiteful nails,*
> *I wept beside that tree.*
> *I hated all who stood and watched*
> *In truth, I hated me.*
>
> *I tried to pray, but bitter tears*
> *Engulfed me in despair.*
> *The end of all we'd hoped for*
> *Was more than I could bear.*
>
> *I know you'd said you'd rise again*
> *But, Lord, I saw you die.*
> *That broken, twisted body.*
> *That desperate, lonely cry.*

Darkness swamped my very soul,
The sky itself turned black
But blacker still was my belief
That you weren't coming back.

My brothers came and found me
They told me what you'd done
How you'd come and stood among them
That you really were God's Son.

Oh, I wanted to believe them
And cast my grief aside
But fear welled up inside me
And doubts too fierce to hide.

'Unless I put my hand in his
And feel the marks of pain
I'll never be convinced,' I said,
'That he's alive again.'

The days went by without a sign
That what they claimed was true
When suddenly you stood there
Saying, 'Peace be unto you.'

My Lord, my God, forgive me,
I don't know what to say
But now I know you are the Son
The Life, the Truth, the Way.

If you are able, visit a church or cathedral and spend time looking at the stained-glass windows. Find one that speaks to you and be drawn into the story it tells, into the lives it portrays.

If you can't travel, take a postcard or a picture of a stained glass window and sit quietly with that image.

Windows of prayer

Creative/intercession

One of my favourite TV programmes when I was a child was *Play School*, particularly the moment when you had to guess which window would open. There was a round window, a square window and an arched window, and each day the camera would pan in, the chosen window would open and a story would unfold.

Using that model, draw three windows on large pieces of paper.

The round window could represent the world. In the window, write situations or stick on newspaper cuttings and pray for places and people in the world.

The square window could be for family and friends. Write their names in the window, or attach their photos and pray for them each in their need and in thankfulness for what they mean to you.

The arched window could be for the church locally, nationally and worldwide. Pray for the coming of God's kingdom and for a reaching out to those who have lost confidence in the church. Pray for the mission of Christ's church today, for courage and humility for leaders and a fresh anointing of the Holy Spirit for all who are the body of Christ today.

Stick the windows up on your wall if you can.

Dangerous or safe?

Reflective/going outside

Windows can be dangerous places—as Eutychus found out when he nodded off listening to Paul preach (Acts 20:7–12). He fell from the third storey and was killed outright. Paul didn't panic; he prayed over the young man and sent him back home alive and safe.

One of the most haunting memories from 9/11 was watching men and women jump out of windows to escape an even more dreadful death in the burning twin towers. While great stories of faith and courage emerged from that tragedy, there wasn't the happy ending of the Acts account. Windows were a place where dreadful decisions were made that day. Perhaps they can be places where we can make big decisions today in our lives.

Open windows can be dangerous; they can be places of escape; they can be safe places as well. Watching thunder and lightning flashing around from behind a bedroom window can bring a great sense of feeling snug and safe. We can watch all the excitement without getting windswept or wet. A pane of glass is all it can take to give us a sense of being protected.

Do we sometimes feel we need to protect ourselves from God? From love? Do we sit behind windows of our own making to keep God at arm's length, to keep our vulnerability and sense of inadequacy hidden behind glass and even curtains? To open the window in a storm would be to experience it, to be enveloped by it. Do we need to open the windows of our hearts and minds to encounter God, to give God more of ourselves?

If you can, sit by an upstairs window and look out. Does it protect you from a hostile environment? Does it give you a sense of feeling separated from all that you look out on? Is it a place of hiding? Does it make you feel safe?

Take a few minutes to think about your relationship with God. When you pray, is there an open or a closed window between you and God? If closed, slowly open it and invite Jesus to join you where you are. If that feels too big a step, name those things that you are afraid of showing to God. What makes you want to hide?

Go and walk in the place you have been looking out on. How different does it feel actually 'being there'?

Windows of surprise

Prayer

Recently I was huddled in my caravan feeling very sorry for myself. It was wet, cold, and night was closing in. Suddenly, in the distance, a rainbow appeared.

A few strands of colour transformed my mood, and I could only marvel at its beauty. It was gone in moment, but it was a wonderful and precious gift to me on that drab, grey afternoon. A special blessing and a way into my prayer time which would otherwise have been one long whinge!

Read Genesis 9:8–17 and pray a rainbow prayer today.

Pray *red* for those who cry out for warmth and acceptance and love.
Pray *blue* for all those for whom life's sky has been darkened by illness and loss.
Pray *green* for those who live in places of drought, whose lives feel barren.
Pray *white* for those who feel soiled by life's experiences, who see no beauty in themselves.

Pray *gold* for those who feel they are life's losers, who feel they haven't achieved anything.

Pray *black* for those who are exhausted and need a safe place to rest for a while.

Pray *purple* for the voiceless and those coming to the end of their lives.

Pray *yellow* for those imprisoned by bars or addictions that they may glimpse a brighter future.

Pray a *rainbow* for all those who feel alone today; for all who have given up hope of ever being surprised or blessed.

Next time you are surprised by unexpected beauty, use the experience to shape your prayers and store it away in your heart to bring out again on a rainy day.

Dreaming dreams

Imaginative/prayer

Sit quietly and use your imagination. Imagine drawing back some curtains, opening a window, and picture exactly what you would most like to see. What would it be? What prayer would you most like to see answered?

What are your most urgent prayers? Of what is our world in most urgent need? It might be that the picture you dream is of a little child laughing, walking hand in hand with another child, and you might pray for the raising up of more Mary and Josephs to love and nurture and protect, and for an end to the tyranny of the Herods of this world, who crush the innocence of childhood. It might be that behind the window is a lamb frolicking in a field and you might pray that all creatures might be blessed with freedom and be safe from cruelty and abuse. You might see a group of people kneading bread together and smiling, and pray for an end to hunger and poverty and for a sharing of the world's resources. You may see a bird gliding in the breeze and pray for freedom for all those trapped and imprisoned.

What dreams are you dreaming?

For yourself?

For the world?

How might you make those dreams begin to come true?

In each moment of time, in each day and each hour, God the Father is waiting for the windows of our longings to be opened to receive his blessing.

In each mind, in each body, Christ is waiting for the windows of our prayers to be opened to receive his blessing.

In each conversation, in each relationship, the Holy Spirit is waiting for the windows of our hearts to be opened to receive blessing and healing.

Quiet Days

Sally Smith

When Jesus saw the crowds, he went up the mountain.
MATTHEW 5:1, NRSV

Some of us head for the mountains at the first sight of a crowd, getting as far away from the hordes of people as possible. Others of us will head straight into the midst of the crowd, anxious to meet and greet everyone if we can. Jesus did both. Sometimes he was in the midst of the crowd, jostled and touched by those around him. At other times he avoided the crowds to find a quiet place on his own or with a few friends. We see in Mark 5:21–34 how being touched by one in search of healing in a crowd could drain Jesus of his power. It was in the quiet places, particularly on the mountains, that he regained that power and prepared for the times ahead. It was in those places that he was in the presence of his heavenly father and it was there that he was able to refocus on his work and ministry.

Do we need to follow Jesus' example and go away to a quiet place, or can we manage with meeting God in our daily lives? For me, the answer is that I need the times away from the distractions that everyday life brings. Sometimes this can be in the form of a retreat: the luxury of several days away with God, in a quiet, usually beautiful, place where I am looked after and I can allow God the space to love me, reassure me, challenge me and then send me back to work for him. But retreats are a luxury many of us cannot afford—in terms of time or of finance—as often as we would like. To some, several days away from the busyness, structure and stability of life may seem too daunting and frightening, triggering a whole series of questions: what happens... what if... who... can I... what do I do? A Quiet Day may be a way of beginning—an opportunity to try a few hours away, in God's presence, without the structures we have come to rely on, a chance to see what it feels like to be totally open to God for a few hours. For those with experience of retreats, a Quiet Day may be a bridge between retreats, giving a top-up that will keep them going until the next retreat.

What can you expect if you sign up for a Quiet Day? Usually there will be some form of opening worship—from a brief time together in the quiet with maybe a psalm or short Bible reading, to a Communion service. There will be an opportunity to meet those with whom you will be spending the day. Usually the aim of the day is not the meeting of others, but allowing time and space to meet with God. Often there will be an address (or series of addresses) about some aspect of prayer or the Christian life. This may be interesting on an academic level, but will have the greatest effect if you allow it to touch you at a deeper level. It is when we allow God to reach deeper that we are changed and enabled to become more like him. It can be easy on a Quiet Day to let our brains take over, to allow them to go into overdrive and analyse what is being shared with us. You might like to try just sitting with what you have heard. Instead of searching hard for what God might be saying to you through the speaker, try sitting still, or taking a very gentle walk, and allowing God to talk to you; allow him the space to say what he wants, not what you think he might want to say. It may be that God wants to say something huge to you, and it is only in the space and safety of a day with him that you will be able to hear and take in what you might be being called to. Or it might be that God simply wants to spend some time with you, to tell you how much and why he loves you, and what he values about you.

It helps not to go with too many expectations of the day. Expecting God to give you the blueprint for the next ten years of your life is unrealistic and doesn't allow him the space to say what is really important. My experience has been that when I have allowed God to set the agenda for the day he has done so, and often it has not been anything like my agenda. God sees our lives differently from the way we see them, and to listen and see through his eyes gives a perspective and focus that can take us to some unexpected places. Or God may just want to spend time with you and to give you rest, allowing you time to recharge your batteries ready for the coming days.

On a Quiet Day there should be some time for you to spend on your own. It is a good idea to make use of this time in being alone, allowing God the space to be with you. It might seem rude or a wasted opportunity not to talk to the other people who are there, but think—why did you come on the day? What do you want to achieve? If your aim is to meet others and have a good chat and put the world to rights, maybe a Quiet Day isn't the best plan; a walking group or meeting friends for a coffee might be a better choice. Sometimes all or part of the Quiet Day will be in silence. This makes ignoring others without seeming rude easier, but brings with it other issues: what if there's an emergency? What if I want to ask a question? Won't eating without talking feel uncomfortable? Yes, to start with it may feel uncomfortable, but you will soon find it enables you to acknowledge the food you are eating, to taste and savour the good gifts you are being offered. It also avoids interruption in what is happening for you internally. Try not to see silent meals as a time to be endured, to feed the body so that you can carry on with the real business of the day. Instead, see it as another opportunity to listen to God, to receive the food he gives, to taste the produce of his creation. You will also find you become sensitive to those around you, aware of their needs and ready to serve them in ways that go unnoticed in the usual noisy bustle of a meal with a group of new friends.

It can be helpful to take a notebook or journal with you, not just to make notes of what the speaker has been talking about, but to reflect on the impact this has on you. What difference will what you have heard make tomorrow or next week? You might want to record what you believe God has been saying to you, and make a response to him. Sometimes writing our prayers to God can help clarify what we are saying, and can be a good reminder in the days ahead of what was happening and how you were feeling and thinking in the time away without the pressures that often distort our thinking the rest of the time.

As you think about going, you might be concerned about what questions you will be asked and whether there will be an expectation to share your experience with everyone else. The rule is always to share as much or as little as you want and feel comfortable with. This might vary; sometimes I am comfortable with sharing much of what has happened during a day, but at other times I need to hold it tight and allow it to sink in, to become part of me, before I am willing to share. It may be very personal and not directly helpful for others, and that's fine. It may be general, which could help others clarify what God has been saying to them and give them an insight into who God is through his work in you. It can be that in the saying aloud what has been happening you become clear in yourself what has been going on, and as you talk you may be aware of the importance of a detail you had previously thought unimportant. If you are offered the opportunity and feel able to, it can be a valuable exercise to talk to one or two others, or the whole group, towards the end of the day, but there is no obligation to do so.

As well as going on an organised Quiet Day, sometimes it can be helpful to go away for a day by yourself. This might be to a favourite place in the country or to stay in a friend's empty house, or to a convent or retreat house, where you will be able to join in the rhythm of prayer of the house and often share a meal with the community. If you go alone, the temptation can be to spend the whole day reading a book (spiritual, rather than a novel). If you find yourself doing this, read it slowly. Allow time for the words to seep in. Stop when you read a sentence that is offering something to you. Stay with that sentence for as long as you are able. Exactly what is the sentence saying to you, and what is God saying to you through the words? Reading slowly in this way, you may find you only read one or two pages in a day, but think of the depth and goodness you will have gained from those pages, and the opportunity you will have given God to speak to you, allowing space to listen. Or you might prefer to take your *Quiet Spaces* with you and work through two or three exercises in detail, taking time that you would not be able to commit during a normal week.

As you come towards the end of the day, it can be helpful to reflect on what has been happening. If you are with a group, you could do this with another person. Listen to them as attentively as you would like to be listened to; treat their experience with the same sensitivity you expect from them. If you are on your own, you might like to write a reminder of what you have been given during the day, or you might prefer to find an image or object that reflects the day, something you can take back with you as a reminder. Before you leave, spend a few minutes recalling the things you have left behind at home—what issues, events, people are you going back to? Are you ready for all they will throw at you as soon as you walk through the door? Are you ready to draw on those new inner resources as you explain what has been happening, maybe even justify the use of the time? Living in a city, I often find the journey to and from a Quiet Day reflects the leaving behind of the busyness and the picking it up again as I return. The first sight of the ring road always marks for me the point of re-entry: from here on I am drawing on the resources gained during the day and am using the inner silence I have refuelled.

As a Child

Phil Steer

Humbles

> *Therefore, whoever humbles himself like this child is the greatest in the kingdom of heaven.*
>
> MATTHEW 18:3, NIV 1984, EMPHASIS MINE

Winston Churchill is reputed to have said of Clement Attlee, the post-war British Prime Minister, that he was 'a modest man, who has much to be modest about.' This was not, of course, intended to be taken as a compliment. Churchill was suggesting not that Attlee had many significant abilities and achievements about which he could be modest, but rather that his abilities and achievements were of such insignificance that modesty was the only appropriate response.

This typically amusing Churchillian put-down hints at what it means to be humble like a child—and this is something rather different from what we adults tend to think of as humility.

For adults, humility generally entails us playing down our abilities and achievements, and setting aside any advantages associated with our position and power. It is, if you like, behaving as if we did not have these things.

Let's be honest, humility such as this is not something that we see very often in little children. In part this is because they are too young to realise the necessity for humility, or even truly to understand what humility is. More to the point, however, is the fact that there is little or nothing in their lives that they are able to play down or set aside, even if they wanted to; for their abilities are limited, their achievements are small, they have no position or power. To mimic Churchill's comment about Attlee, they are humble and they have much to be humble about.

As such, the humility of a little child is not so much an attitude of mind as a state of being, a fundamental part of who and what they are. Indeed, the word 'humble' can literally mean 'not rising far from the ground', which is a perfect way to describe these 'little ones', whose size dictates a very real physical humility: small, and powerless and weak.

In their letters, both Paul and Peter exhort the early believers to 'clothe yourselves with humility' (1 Peter 5:5; Colossians 3:12). This phrase is suggestive of what it means for adults to be humble: it is something that we 'put on'—at best, from a desire not to 'show off' what we are and what we have: at worst, simply to cover over our pride.

In contrast, childlike humility is not so much a 'putting on' as a 'putting off'; a giving up of our desire to have and our desire to be; a giving up, even, of what we have and what we are. To be truly humble like a child is to have few possessions, a lowly position, little power.

For this was the way taken by Jesus. His humility entailed an actual, physical change in his circumstances, a very real 'coming down'. His was the greatness and the power and the glory and the majesty and the splendour of God (1 Chronicles 29:11). He had everything, yet he made himself nothing; he chose freely to give it all up, to let it all go. He set aside his divinity to take on our humanity. Leaving his eternal home with his Father in heaven, he came to live a life here on earth: a life of service and of obedience and ultimately of death on a cross (Philippians 2:5–8).

And he came as a helpless baby, totally dependent upon his human parents for protection and provision, for all that he needed to survive and to grow. We are so familiar with this story that we seldom feel any shock at the idea of almighty God making himself so vulnerable; we can hardly envisage things happening any other way. And yet Jesus could just as easily have appeared on earth as a fully grown man, ready to embark upon his adult ministry. Instead, he chose to share the full extent of our humanity and to show the endless depths of his humility, by becoming a little child.

Such an understanding of humility could have a profound effect on how we live out our faith. Many Christians and many churches desire to do something 'significant' for God—and, of course, this is in many ways a laudable aim. But what this can translate to in practice is a desire to become significant ourselves: to gain more prominence and to increase our influence—not, of course, for our own sakes (perish the thought!), but rather that we might be better equipped to 'impact' the world for God.

Now there is no doubt that there are individuals and churches that are called upon by God to take on such 'significant' roles: to be high-profile, to be influential, to be 'successful'—and far be it from me to call into question the reality of any such calling. I would, however, question whether this is the path that God wants most of us to take. In his letter to the church in Corinth, Paul tells us about the type of person that God chooses and uses to fulfil his purposes. And rarely is it those whom the world would consider to be wise or influential or important; rather, it's the foolish and the weak and the lowly and the despised. He chooses 'the things that are not... so that none may boast before him' (1 Corinthians 1:26–29).

What a telling phrase this is! We want to be 'something', yet God chooses those who are 'nothing'. We fondly believe that the more we bring to God, the more he will be able to use us. But God doesn't need us to bring him anything; indeed, it seems he would almost prefer it if we didn't. For he is the One who delights in creating something out of nothing; who in the beginning spoke into the darkness and brought forth the heavens and the earth. How much more, then, is he able to produce whatever he desires from the 'nothingness' of our lives. As others have said, the only ability that God requires of us is availability.

Speaking to his disciples of his impending death, Jesus said to them, 'I tell you the truth, unless a kernel of wheat falls to the ground and dies, it remains only a single seed. But if it dies, it produces many seeds' (John 12:24). Fruitfulness and abundance, it seems, must come through humility and death: first and foremost through the death of Jesus, then through each of us dying to our own selfish ambitions and desires. Just as a seed is literally humbled in falling to the ground and entering the soil, so we in humbling ourselves come into that place from which true growth and increase will come. And throughout history there have been countless men and women of faith—the vast majority known only to God—who have done just this, and whose lives of humble service have been the channels through which God has touched and transformed the lives of individuals, families, communities, countries, even the whole world.

The kingdom of God is an upside-down kingdom, a topsy-turvy kingdom: where the first are last, and the last are first (Mark 9:35); where the one who rules is like the one who serves (Luke 22:26); where those who seem to be weaker are indispensable (1 Corinthians 12:22); where those who exalt themselves will be humbled, and those who humble themselves will be exalted (Matthew 23:12); where the greatest is a little child (18:4). If we truly desire to 'make a difference for God' and see his kingdom come, then we need to do things God's way and not the world's way. There is no need for us to try and ape its attitudes or mimic its methods. Nor do we need to compete with the world in order to try to prove God's power, with an attitude of 'Anything you can do, God can do better.' Rather, we need to learn to walk the way of 'insignificance', seeking to be 'nothing' rather than desiring to be 'something', learning to love and serve in gentleness and humility. If we are willing to do this, then God himself will take care of any 'significance' in what we do. After all, in the seeming insignificance and failure of his earthly life and death, Jesus achieved something of the greatest significance for all humanity, whose effect will be felt throughout all eternity.

Spotlight:
The Sisters of Bethany

Mother Rita-Elizabeth, SSB

'You want us to offer monastic worship at Greenbelt?' we queried incredulously. 'Yes,' they said, 'lots of people will want it as an alternative!'

'Nuns on Twitter and Facebook?' they wondered. 'Yes,' we said, 'that's where lots of people are looking for interaction with others and we will communicate interaction with God!'

'Retreats for women?' they ridiculed our Mother Foundress in 1866. 'Yes,' she said, 'there is a need!'

'You are going to found a community to pray for Christian unity?' they challenged Mother Foundress. 'Yes,' she insisted, 'It is the Lord's will!'

And so it is that we enjoy fellowship with all people in prayer and worship to the glory of God and in response to what we believe to be God's will for us. We live in community as Sisters of Bethany under the vows of poverty, chastity and obedience. These traditional monastic vows give expression to the liberty that comes from being freed from some of the constraints of contemporary culture. The vow of poverty commits us to live in simplicity and gratitude, avoiding extravagance and wastefulness, holding material possessions in common and sharing what we have been given with those in need. The vow of chastity frees us from an exclusive bond and so allows us to relate to others in love which is undemanding and respects the integrity of the other, being rooted in love of God. The vow of obedience expresses our intention to lead a disciplined life, freed from the tyranny of self-will, rooted in a desire to fulfil God's will for us—finding guidance principally in the scriptures and the shared discernment of the community. The three vows give a framework to help each of us in our own search for union with God, and within which we can check our contribution to and participation in the communal life. Taken as a whole, the vows are a significant source of strength in times of difficulty, when we recall that the profession of those vows was the sacramental sign of a covenant made with God and the receiving of the blessing of his grace.

Our main work is corporate worship. Our Rule calls us to the unceasing praise we owe to God in acknowledgement of his supreme majesty and entire claim on our life—and it reminds us that we stand before God on behalf of the world. The offices (or short services) we celebrate each day are known as the Divine Office. The Divine Office provides an annual, weekly and daily rhythm which reflects the life of Christ. At the beginning of the church's year, we celebrate the incarnation of Jesus with a period of preparation during Advent, leading to the celebration of Christmas and its fulfilment during the Epiphany season. Then we enter the second part of the year, which celebrates our redemption with a period of preparation during Lent, leading to the celebration of Easter and its fulfilment in the season of Ascension, and the period following Pentecost, in which we explore God the Holy Trinity's work in Christ through the life of the Church.

Each week begins with the eve of Sunday and the weekly feast of our Lord's resurrection. On a daily basis the fixed hours for Mattins, Terce, Midday Office, Vespers and Compline find us in chapel each day reciting words of scripture hallowed by our Lord's own use and that of the people of God throughout the ages. The daily Eucharist is at the centre of our liturgy and life. Feeding on Christ by faith and with thanksgiving in word and sacrament, we are being transformed into his likeness and made one with each other in him. Our day starts with Mattins as a daily celebration of passing from darkness to light and an emphasis on praise. Terce commends the day and all our activities to the guidance of God the Holy Spirit, and the Midday Office offers the service of our lives and our intercessions for the needs of the world. Vespers marks the end of the day's work and is traditionally the start of the new day with the Magnificat, which celebrates the incarnation. At Compline we invoke God's blessing through the night and long for the final fulfilment of God's kingdom. Many who have visited us and experienced the Divine Office find that they can make one or more of the Offices part of their own daily prayer time.

Through social media and personal contacts come the many prayer requests that we offer together each day within the Midday Office. We watch the TV news after lunch each day to inform our prayers. Daily prayers are offered for Christian unity. Also, we each have a period of time for personal prayer and spiritual reading each day.

This pattern forms the framework for our work of hospitality and fellowship with our visitors. Set in suburban Southsea, it is easy to reach us by train, bus and ferry—we are accessible. We have accommodation for guests who live 'as family' with us. We welcome guests for Julian prayer groups, Quiet Days and Quiet Afternoons and a 'Bethany Group' for discussion, as well as to stay for a retreat or quiet holiday.

Living as a family in Christ and in the power of the Spirit, we love and serve God and one another after the example of Martha, Mary and Lazarus. We are pilgrims on a journey that we love to share with others.

For more information about the Sisters of Bethany visit
Website: www.sistersofbethany.org.uk
Email: ssb@sistersofbethany.org.uk
Twitter: www.twitter.com/bethanysister
Facebook: www.facebook.com/sisters.ofbethany

BRF Quiet Days

BRF Quiet Days are an ideal way of redressing the balance in our busy lives. Held in peaceful locations around the country, each one is led by an experienced speaker and gives the opportunity to reflect, be silent and pray, and through it all to draw closer to God.

Monday 2 March: 'Living from the Still Centre' led by Jennifer Rees Larcombe at The House of Retreat, The Street, Pleshey, Chelmsford, Essex, CM3 1HA

Wednesday 11 March: 'Deep Calls to Deep' led by Tony Horsfall at The Mirfield Centre, Stocks Bank Road, Mirfield, West Yorkshire, WF14 0BN

Thursday 30 April: 'He isn't heavy, he's my brother' led by Adrian and Bridget Plass at Scargill House, Kettlewell, nr Skipton, North Yorkshire, BD23 5HU

For further details and to book, and for information about Quiet Days later in 2015, please go to www.brfonline.org.uk/events-and-quiet-days or contact us at BRF, 15 The Chambers, Vineyard, Abingdon, Oxfordshire, OX14 3FE; tel: 01865 319700.

Quiet Spaces Subscription

Please note one-year subscription prices below include postage and packing.

You can also purchase your subcription by Direct Debit. Complete the details on the direct debit form and post to BRF with the order form.

Please send *Quiet Spaces* beginning with the May 2015/September 2015/ January 2016 issue (delete as applicable).

PRICES FOR UK ADDRESSES

DESCRIPTION	PRICE	QUANTITY ORDERED	TOTAL
Individual 1-year subscription includes postage and packing	£16.35		
Group 1-year subscription postage and packing FREE	£12.90		
ORDER TOTAL			

PRICES FOR OVERSEAS ADDRESSES—INCLUDES POSTAGE & PACKING

DESCRIPTION	PRICE	QUANTITY ORDERED	TOTAL
Individual 1-year subscription Standard	£27.60		
Individual 1-year subscription Europe and economy	£24.00		
ORDER TOTAL			

Prices are correct at time of going to press and subject to change.
For information about group subscriptions, see overleaf or contact BRF at the address given on the next page.

Promo code: QS0115

Method of payment

☐ Cheque ☐ MasterCard ☐ Maestro ☐ Visa ☐ Postal Order

Card no. ☐☐☐☐☐ ☐☐☐☐☐ ☐☐☐☐☐ ☐☐☐☐☐ ☐☐☐

Shaded boxes for Maestro use only

Valid from ☐☐☐☐ Expires ☐☐☐☐ Issue No. (Switch only) ☐☐☐☐

Security code* ☐☐☐ (Last 3 digits on the reverse of the card *Essential in order to process your order*) 0000 **000** EXAMPLE

Signature .... Date ...... / ...... / ....

All subscription orders must be accompanied by the appropriate payment.
Please note: do not send payments for group orders. All group orders will be invoiced.

Name ....

Acc. No. ....

Address...

....

.... Postcode ....

Telephone...

Email...

If you and a minimum of four friends subscribe to *Quiet Spaces* or BRF's other Bible reading notes (*New Daylight, Day by Day with God, Guidelines, The Upper Room*), you can form a group. What's so good about being in a group? You pay the price of the notes only—postage is free for delivery to a UK address. (All notes are sent to one address.) All group orders are invoiced. No advance payment is required. For more information, see www.biblereadingnotes.org.uk/group-subscriptions/ or contact the BRF office.

BRF, 15 The Chambers, Vineyard, Abingdon OX14 3FE;
Tel: 01865 319700   Fax: 01865 319701
www.brf.org.uk   email: enquiries@brf.org.uk
BRF is a Registered Charity (no: 233280)

Direct Debit

You can pay for your annual subscription to BRF notes using Direct Debit. You need to give your bank details only once, and the payment is made automatically every year until you cancel it. If you would like to pay by Direct Debit, please use the form opposite, entering your BRF account number under 'Reference'.

You are fully covered by the Direct Debit Guarantee:

The Direct Debit Guarantee

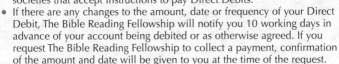

- This Guarantee is offered by all banks and building societies that accept instructions to pay Direct Debits.
- If there are any changes to the amount, date or frequency of your Direct Debit, The Bible Reading Fellowship will notify you 10 working days in advance of your account being debited or as otherwise agreed. If you request The Bible Reading Fellowship to collect a payment, confirmation of the amount and date will be given to you at the time of the request.
- If an error is made in the payment of your Direct Debit, by The Bible Reading Fellowship or your bank or building society, you are entitled to a full and immediate refund of the amount paid from your bank or building society.
  - If you receive a refund you are not entitled to, you must pay it back when The Bible Reading Fellowship asks you to.
- You can cancel a Direct Debit at any time by simply contacting your bank or building society. Written confirmation may be required. Please also notify us.

The Bible Reading Fellowship

Instruction to your bank or
building society to pay by Direct Debit

Please fill in the whole form using a ballpoint pen and send to The Bible
Reading Fellowship, 15 The Chambers, Vineyard, Abingdon OX14 3FE.

Service User Number: | 5 | 5 | 8 | 2 | 2 | 9 |

Name and full postal address of your bank or building society

To: The Manager ....

.... Bank/Building Society

Address ....

....

.... Postcode ....

Name(s) of account holder(s)

Branch sort code

☐☐ – ☐☐ – ☐☐

Bank/Building Society account no.

☐☐☐☐☐☐☐☐

Reference

☐☐☐☐☐☐☐☐

Instruction to your Bank/Building Society

Please pay The Bible Reading Fellowship Direct Debits from the account
detailed in this instruction, subject to the safeguards assured by the Direct
Debit Guarantee. I understand that this instruction may remain with The
Bible Reading Fellowship and, if so, details will be passed electronically to
my bank/building society.

Signature(s)

....

Date

Banks and Building Societies may not accept Direct Debit instructions for
some types of account.